Coffee Wisdom

Coffee Wisdom

7 Finely-Ground Principles for Living a Full-Bodied Life

Theresa Cheung

CONARI PRESS

First published in 2003 by Conari Press,
an imprint of Red Wheel/Weiser, LLC
York Beach, ME
With offices at:
368 Congress Street
Boston, MA 02210
www.redwheelweiser.com

Library of Congress Cataloging-in-Publication Data

Cheung, Theresa.
  Coffee wisdom / Theresa Cheung.
      p. cm.
  ISBN 1-57324-865-7
  1. Coffee brewing. 2. Cookery (Coffee) 3. Coffee. 1. Title.
  TX817.C6C47 2003
  641.6'373--dc21

                                        2003014028

Typeset in RotisSemiSerif
Printed in Canada
Printer TCP
10 09 08 07 06 05 04 03
8 7 6 5 4 3 2 1

This book is dedicated to my inspiration and the true source of my success, my coffee-loving soul mate, Ray.

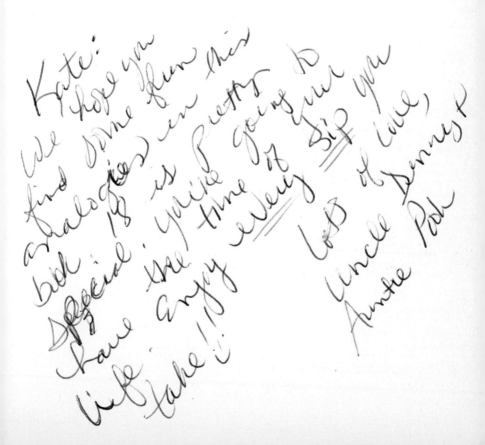

Kate:
We hope you
find some humor
analogies in this
book : is pretty
special : you're going to
have the time of your
life. enjoy every sip you
take !!!
                    Lots of love,
                    Uncle Denny &
                    Auntie Pah

Acknowledgments

Thank you to Jan and everyone at Red Wheel/Weiser/Conari for believing in this book right from the start. Thank you to my partner, Ray, and our fantastic children, Robert and Ruth. I couldn't have completed this project without your support, love, and enthusiasm. Thanks to my brother Terry and his partner, Robin. Thanks to Judy Chilcote for her advice and input. Thanks to Shirley May (Shirley@indexing.co.uk) for her lovely illustrations. Finally, special thanks to Cheryl Kimball for her help and support with this project and to Dr. Priscilla Stuckey for her wit, insight, and fine developmental editing.

Contents

Introduction

Coffee has long been one of life's subtle pleasures; few drinks are as satisfying, comforting, and stimulating.

In eighteenth-century London, the coffeehouses were often known as "penny universities"—you paid a penny to enter and two pennies for the coffee and a paper. Those with an inquiring mind could sit down with poets, merchants, and tinkers and exchange opinions over a cup of coffee. The coffeehouses were places for freedom of speech and thought.

Centuries later, coffee drinking still gives the stimulus to clear thought all over the world. A cup of coffee is a call to action, the lubricant of great thoughts, conversation, and celebration. Research from the University of California in San Diego backs this up. Studies suggest that a lifetime cup of coffee a day improves memory and heightens mental alertness and arousal. Small wonder, then, that coffee is still the favorite drink for every student of life.

It was after one of those chats over a cup of coffee that many of us have had about the philosophies of life and the universe and everything that I started to think about the intoxicating, heartwarming, and utterly pleasurable drink I was holding in my hand.

Some meditate for hours searching for inner peace. Others can find it instantly. Serenity, tranquility, and balance are all right here in my coffee cup. When I'm enjoying coffee, I'm not trying to be or do anything. I'm simply being myself. Coffee gives me energy and time to chill out, and makes me feel good. What can I learn from this? When I'm enjoying my coffee, I'm simply enjoying the moment—a guiding principle for a contented life perhaps?

That's what gave me the idea: to write a book that related the principles of a happy, contented life to enjoying a perfect cup of coffee. The seven principles of coffee wisdom are as rich, enlightening, and invigorating as the beverage they celebrate. Whether you decide to dip into or read this book from cover to cover, the positive reflections, practical strategies, and inspirational techniques are all designed to help you stay fully awake, live life to the maximum, and feel good every day. It goes without saying that drinking a delicious cup or two as you read or reread this book is of course highly recommended.

The Seven Principles of Coffee Wisdom

1. **Reheating causes bitterness.**
   Your past is the reason, not the excuse.

2. **Start with fresh grounds.**
   Learn from your mistakes, don't repeat them.

3. **Use the correct grind.**
   Put right what you can and accept what you can't.

4. **Use high-quality beans and fresh, pure, cold water.**
   Celebrate your uniqueness.

5. **Get the proportions right.**
   Challenge irrational thinking.

6. **Boiling destroys the flavor.**
   Check your stress levels.

7. **Drink it while it's hot.**
   Live in the present.

Principle #1

Reheating Causes Bitterness

About Coffee:
Coffee should not be reheated. Every time you brew a cup, it needs to be fresh. Make only as much as you plan to drink.

About Life:
Don't rehash the past. Your past is the reason, not the excuse. Let go of what is gone.

If you reheat coffee it won't taste good. It's the same with your life. Rehashing the past will bring a bad taste to your life. For happy, contented living, take responsibility in the now, and move forward from this moment.

:: Life Is Yours for the Tasting

The morning cup of coffee has an exhilaration about it which the cheering influence of the afternoon or evening cup can not be expected to reproduce.
—Dr. Oliver Wendell Holmes, writer and physician

Make sure the coffee you drink is always fresh. The split-second, stop-action pleasure that comes with that first sip will remind you that every day is a fresh chance to make important changes in your life. Every day you can start over.

You can't change what has been done or said. Let the past go. Remember that you did the very best that you could do at the time and now look forward to a positive future. Understand your past; don't use it as an excuse. If you feel you have behaved badly or made mistakes, then apologize and try to make things right. When you have done the best that you can do, accept responsibility and move forward.

Stop blaming yourself. Everyone makes mistakes. Learn from them, understand your motivations, and seize the initiative to make changes in your life. If you are feeling bad about your love life, do something about it. Find ways to meet people. Be friendly. Ask other people out. They may not know how great you are. If you need a better job, don't wait for the perfect one to find you. Go after it. Having a can-do attitude isn't being aggressive and pushy—it is simply being enthusiastic, enterprising, and resourceful.

To be happy, you don't need to succeed in everything you do, but you do need to believe that you have control over your life. Research suggests that those who feel they are responsible for their own decisions are often more satisfied with their lives than those who do not. People are happiest when they allow their individual personality to express itself, not when they try to conform to someone else's identity.

Don't wait for others to set the pace. Be a leader. Don't wait for opportunity to find you. Seek it out. Happy people are not necessarily more talented than anyone else, but they usually get what they want because they seek opportunities, not guarantees. They don't wait for incentives but are constantly alert to what is going on around them. They know that every situation holds the seed of opportunity, and when it appears they are prepared to let go of the past and take action to create a better future. Every day is full of golden opportunities. Every day is fresh and new and happy. Contented people make sure they taste every moment.

::COFFEE BOX: The Method::

The great pleasure of making coffee is that it is not complicated as long as you stick to the same measurements. Whether you use a jug, a cafetiere (French press), or a coffee sock, use the freshest grounds and freshly run water that boiled five seconds ago. Coffee should never touch boiling water and should never be boiled again. Don't use hot milk unless you can steam-heat it in an espresso machine—when you use heated milk, you risk tainting the coffee with the taste of caramelized sugars. Better to store your cups in a warm place to keep the warmth in the coffee.

:: Five Ways to Ruin Your Coffee:

- Adding overheated milk. Be sure that the milk is warm, not boiling.
- Reheating your coffee by bringing it back to a boil.
- Mixing old coffee with new in a jar.
- Overmeasuring—you won't make stronger coffee by adding more grains. Buy a stronger roast.
- Using boiling water—it makes the coffee bitter.

:: What's Gone Wrong?

Coffee tastes dull. Use fresh, cold water—let the tap run for a while before you fill the kettle. Pour the boiled water onto the coffee five seconds after it has boiled, but don't leave it. Fifteen seconds' delay can make all the difference between dull and great-tasting coffee.

Coffee looks gray. You have chosen too dark a roast. For a milky coffee, you need a full-flavored variety such as a Colombia or a Java.

Coffee tastes bitter. It could be a cheap coffee, containing Robusta. Try pure Arabica instead. You may also have used too much coffee or added boiling water or milk.

:: No More Excuses

Your past is the reason not the excuse. Stop regretting what has happened and wish that you had done something different. You can look back and regret your actions but you cannot change the past. All you can do is understand and learn from it. Blaming yourself or others for things that didn't go well is only going to turn your spirit bitter. Bitter coffee can't work its comfort and magic, and neither can a bitter spirit. Don't keep turning the past over and over again in your mind; it won't accomplish anything and will only make you feel powerless.

The past is there to be understood, not dwelled on. Understand why you behaved a certain way. What were your reasons? What were your motivations? What part did you play in creating your present circumstances? Accept responsibility and let go. Let yourself off the hook. We all make mistakes. Learn from them and move on.

Start with today. Excuses won't help you move forward with your life. Excuses are those little voices in our heads telling us we can't do something because of what happened in the past. So leave the past behind and take action in the present. Ever notice how motivated people become when they are diagnosed with a terminal illness? Don't wait for that shock before you pursue the life of your dreams.

In one year, Anthony Burgess finished five novels. What motivated him was being told he had only six months to live. He had no money to leave to his wife, and writing was all he could think to do to leave any kind of security for his family.

But Anthony Burgess did not die. His cancer went into remission and then disappeared. In his long and full life, Burgess wrote seventy books. Without the death sentence from cancer at age forty, he might never have written anything.

You don't need a death sentence to start doing the things you have always wanted to do with your life. You can do them all right now. Take a coffee break, and list five things you would do differently in the next six months if you thought you had only a year to live. If you are finding it hard to break from routine, don't try to change everything at once. Do just one thing differently, and as you start feeling refreshed this will motivate you to further action.

Remember your past is the reason, not the excuse. Regret, guilt, and blame drag you back into the past and do nothing to improve your present situation. Let your past go, and look forward to a positive future.

:: Wake up and Smell the Coffee

The first principle of coffee wisdom is take responsibility for your life. This encourages you to be proactive.

Every day we have many chances to choose between being proactive or reactive. The weather is bad, you get a disappointment at work, you miss the train, you get a parking ticket or spill your coffee. So, how do you respond? Do you fly off the handle? Do you shout and scream? Or do you make a decision to deal with what comes up and move on? The choice is yours.

Reactive people make choices on impulse. They are like trees blown in the wind. If the wind gets strong, they break. Proactive people think first and then act. They recognize that they can't always control what happens to them, but they can control the way they react. They'd rather spend their lives feeling calm than feeling upset. They don't let other people or things ruin their day.

Has this ever happened to you? One of your friends meets you for a chat and coffee only when her partner is out of town. You feel like you are being used to keep her company when her partner is away.

Reactive choices:

Tell her you think she is selfish and insensitive.

Get depressed.

Give her the cold shoulder.

Tell everyone that she isn't a good friend.

Proactive choices:

Confront her calmly and tell her how you feel.

Forgive her.

Give her a second chance, understanding that she has weaknesses just like you and that you may sometimes neglect your friends without realizing it.

You can usually tell when you are being reactive by the language you use. "That's just the way I am" is typical reactive language. What it really means is, "I have no responsibility for the way I am. I can't change." When you say, "If he or she hadn't done that, things would be different," what you are really saying is someone else is the cause of your problems. When you say, "You just made me feel bad," what you are really saying is, "I am not in control. You are." When you say, "If only I had lived somewhere else, been in another job, had more money," and so on, what you are really saying is, "I am not in control of my happiness, things are. I'm a victim. Everyone has it in for me, and the world owes me something."

Notice that reactive language takes power away from you and gives it to someone else or something else. It's like saying, "You are in charge of my mood. Do with it what you like." Proactive language, on the other hand, gives control back to you. You are then free to choose how you behave. Reactive language: That's just the way I am. There is nothing I can do. I have to. Proactive Language: I'll do it. I can do better than that. Let's consider the options. I choose to.

Voltaire, who was said to have consumed fifty cups of coffee a day, likened life to a game of cards. Each player must accept the cards life deals him or her. But once the cards are in our hands, each of us must decide how to play them in order to win the game. You can't always control what happens to you, but you can control how you choose to respond. You can make excuses, or you can take control. The choice is yours.

:: Attitude

The Boston Tea Party should have been called the Boston Coffee Break because it prompted America to turn its back on tea leaves and embrace the shiny bean.

Have you ever thought you were right about something and then found out that you were completely wrong? Sometimes finding out a bit more information about something or someone can completely change your perspective. You suddenly start seeing things in a new way, as if you have just bought a new pair of contact lenses. For example, you think your friend is moody because you have offended, but her moodiness has nothing to do with you and everything to do with her financial worries.

Just as we have views about other people, which can often be wrong, we also have ideas about ourselves that are out of whack. Think of all those limiting perceptions we have of ourselves such as: I'm no good at this, I can't do that, and I'm not like that. Why not surprise yourself, change your attitude, and do something today that totally contradicts that?

To change your attitude, you need to be willing to shock yourself out of old, limiting attitudes. What kind of a person do you think you are? Do you think there are lots of things "wrong" with you? Most of the negative beliefs you hold about yourself have no foundation in reality. You are not really unkind, selfish, stupid, no good, and so on. You learned your beliefs about yourself many years ago when you believed everything that you heard. If, for example, you were told that you were stupid when you were small, you may still have that belief now. You may be very clever, but deep down you believe that you are stupid. This negative belief colors your whole life, and you will doubt yourself until you can change your negative beliefs.

Let go of negative self-beliefs and be willing to embrace new, freeing attitudes. Train your mind to believe positive things instead. It really is that simple. For example, instead of believing that you are stupid, contradict this by telling yourself you are clever. Say it as many times as you can remember to. Write it down in your diary. Sing it on the way to work. Keep saying it until you start to believe it.

Positive thinking really does work. Don't believe me? Why not give it a try. Just keep telling yourself good things. What have you got to lose? Just a lifetime of negativity and low self-esteem.

You may well find that moving beyond old, limiting attitudes is the coffee wisdom principle that is the hardest to live by. It's tough breaking old habits. It's tough living life in the here and now. So don't get discouraged if you struggle. Here are a few tips:

Don't wait until you are better at doing things until you do them. Put your coffee cup down, leave your insecurities behind, and have a go now.

Be a good role model for your loved ones. Do you want your children or family or friends to learn confidence or insecurity from you? Let them see you moving forward with optimism, not endlessly rehashing the past.

Go through your closet and throw out your old clothes. Are you hanging onto them because of past memories? If so you may find it hard to look ahead because a part of you is still stuck in the past.

Learn to accept all your feelings, don't hide them away. It is okay to feel angry, sad, jealous, and all the other emotions you may think of as "bad." You can't look to the future unless you acknowledge your feelings, feel them, and let them go.

Don't take yourself too seriously. Get in touch with your child-ish playfulness and sense of wonder and optimism. Try out new things, shout, laugh, and bring everything back into perspective.

Principle #2

Start with Fresh Grounds

About Coffee:
Do not reuse grounds. You'll only end up with bitter and unpleasant tastes.

About Life:
Learn from your mistakes, don't repeat them.

Learn from your mistakes. Don't get bitter about or use them as an excuse to stop trying. Turn rejection and disappointment into resolve and direction.

:: Spilling the Beans

Have you ever done something you didn't like and ended up doing it again? Have you ever ended up doing or saying things and have no idea why you are doing them? You drink too much alcohol at a party even though you know you have an important meeting the next morning. You lose your temper with someone even though you know it will just make things worse.

This is where the second principle of coffee wisdom comes in: do not reuse grounds. It's like revisiting a past lover. Everything that was great has already been savored.

If you are repeating behavior that you know isn't good for you-fighting with friends, smoking, losing your cool—then perhaps there is something you are getting out of it. The secret to changing your behavior may be to find out what that payoff is. What is really going on inside you to make you want to do something that is going to make you unhealthy or unhappy? If you can find that out, then you are well on the way to breaking the pattern.

The hidden comfort behind negative or self-destructive behavior can be physical, emotional, mental, or psychological. For example, if you raise your voice at loved ones, the immediate benefit is that you vent your frustration. If you jump from one relationship to another, the payoff is the adrenaline rush you get with a new passion. If you are a cynic, the immediate payoff is not having to show your true feelings. If you are a couch potato, the immediate benefit is not getting too involved in life.

Have a good think about what the payoff is that motivates frustrating and negative behavior patterns in your life. Just by turning the spotlight on these hidden comforts, you can start to take a fresh look at yourself and make better decisions. For example, if you are shy because you are frightened of failing, you can tell yourself that you don't want fear to rule your life. Weigh up the pros and cons of the situation. Is the immediate comfort you get from hiding away worth the long-term damage to your self-esteem? If you shout at people you love when you lose your temper, you can find other ways to vent your feelings.

Until you find out why you do things you don't like, you can't stop doing them. Find out what the hidden comforts behind your negative behavior are. Then, try to understand what is going on in your life. Ignore the hidden benefits, and you will pay in the long run. Don't put up with stale coffee. Throw it out and make a fresh cup. Don't keep doing things that you know aren't helpful. Understand why you are doing them, and you are well on your way to a life that is vivid and fresh.

:: Turn Rejection into Resolve

Nancy Astor: "Winston, if I were married to you, I'd put poison in your coffee."

Winston Churchill: "Nancy if you were my wife, I'd drink it."

—E. Langhorne, *Nancy Astor and Her Friends*

No is an awful word to hear. It can make you cry, raise your voice to people you care about, bury your head under the covers, sleep until noon, eat a whole box of chocolates, or sit in a stupor watching daytime TV. Funny, though, you'd think we would be used to disappointment by now. It is estimated that by the time we're eighteen we have probably heard the word no at least 150,000 times. Setbacks are going to happen in life. Some things don't work out the way we want them to.

So how do you respond when life gives you a thumbs down? Do you get depressed? Do you give up? Do you feel sorry for yourself? Do you feel bitter? Do you blame yourself? Or do you try a new approach? Remember, reused coffee grounds will give your coffee an unpleasant and bitter taste. Time to toss out those old, used-up attitudes and start afresh.

The first thing to do is to stop blaming yourself. Blame and guilt leave you trapped in the past. Discard them like used coffee grounds. Although it is important to accept the part you played when setbacks occur, don't delude yourself into thinking that disappointments are always your fault. People who are happy with themselves take defeat and treat it as an isolated incident that indicates nothing about their ability. People who are unhappy take defeat and enlarge it, making it stand for who they are and using it to predict the future of their life. Rejection spells failure only if you do not believe in yourself. For those who believe in themselves, it is only a challenge. So, accept yourself as you are. Don't try to be perfect. You are just like everyone else, a mix of abilities and limitations. Accepting yourself does not mean ignoring your faults or not taking any responsibility; it means believing in your own value, even when you make mistakes.

The hardest rejection to overcome is often self-rejection. If you can see clearly where you went wrong, use that information and move on. But if you don't know what you did wrong, perhaps everything isn't your fault. Disagreements with partners, friends, and family or disappointments at work may have nothing do with what you have said or done. Don't take it personally.

The next time you are rejected, resist the temptation to blame yourself, and try to find out what went wrong. Why didn't you succeed? The answer could help you change your approach. Then, you can try again, using what you have found out. Reflecting on life's disappointments helps you discover other ways to improve your chances of success. Remember, you need to learn from your mistakes, not become obsessed with them.

Find out what went wrong so you can do better next time. Look to your future and let guilt, blame, sadness, and bitterness go. When you feel disappointed—and you will, because mistakes and set-backs can and do happen—acknowledge the losses and then move on. Getting through the tough times will help you learn and grow.

:: Try, Try, Try Again

If you have made a great-tasting cup of coffee, you wouldn't throw it away before you finished it. So, why give up on yourself if things don't immediately go your way? If you believe you have something of value to offer, don't let discouragement slow you down. Keep moving toward the future that is yours by being will-ing to pick yourself up, even after rejection, and try again.

You need only one person to say yes. If at first you don't succeed, welcome to the club. You are in excellent company. The Beatles, Madonna, J. K. Rowling, and Steven Speilberg, to name but a few, all faced major setbacks when they started out. Many successful people with great ideas were rejected by absolutely everybody—except one person. And it was that one acceptance that turned their fortunes around. It doesn't matter how many people say no, if you can find one who says yes; you must simply keep searching for that one.

Being successful means being resilient. It means worrying less about failing and more about the chances you will miss when you don't even try. Many of the people we admire failed many times. Albert Einstein didn't talk until he was four. Beethoven's music teacher said, "As a composer he is hopeless." When Thomas Edison's experiments with a storage battery failed to produce good results, the inventor refused to concede defeat. He said, "I've just found 10,000 ways that won't work!"

Every lasting success involves overcoming rejection. When you adopt this attitude, rejection isn't so frightening anymore. It is a step on the road to success. Be persistent in a creative way. If you truly want something, you will find ways to get it. Don't give up. Believe in yourself. Keep looking for the house, the relationship, the job, the publisher, or whatever of your dreams.

You never know what the future holds. If you feel that life is passing you by and things just aren't going your way, don't despair. Remember, disappointments are an inevitable stepping stone on the road to success. Consider the experiences of:

Harrison Ford: Harrison Ford failed philosophy in his senior year at college in Wisconsin and never received his degree. Following a forty-five-second role in his first movie **Dead Heat on a Merry Go Round**, a Columbia executive told him, "You ain't got it, kid." After bit parts in **Gunsmoke** and **The Virginian**, Ford quit acting for a while and became a carpenter. Later, Ford became a superstar in the **Star Wars** and **Indiana Jones** movies. He also starred in the films **Blade Runner, Witness, Patriot Games, The Fugitive,** and **Air Force One.**

The Beatles: The Beatles were rejected in 1962 by Decca Records executive Dick Rowe, who signed Brian Poole and the Tremeloes instead, following back-to-back auditions by both groups. The Beatles' Decca audition tape was subsequently turned down by Philips, Columbia, and HMV. The Beatles were finally offered a recording contract by Parlophone producer George Martin, and they became the most influential rock 'n' roll band in history.

Walt Disney: Walt Disney's first cartoon company, Laughogram, went bankrupt. Walt Disney subsequently created Mickey Mouse and became the most famous name in film animation. He produced **Snow White and the Seven Dwarfs, Pinocchio, Fantasia, Bambi,** and **Cinderella** and founded Disneyland and Disney World.

Martin Luther King, Jr.: was forced, at age fourteen, to surrender his bus seat to a white passenger and stand for the next ninety miles. King became leader of the American civil rights movement and delivered his famous "I Have a Dream" speech on the steps of the Lincoln Memorial in Washington, DC, before an audience of more than 200,000 people in 1963. He was awarded the Nobel Peace Prize in 1964.

It is encouraging and inspiring to know that anyone who is anyone has had to look rejection in the face and spit in its eye. You can too. Everyone falls down. You are a failure only if you don't get back up.

:: How Do You Like Your Coffee?

"What do you call a large, low-fat latte made with a decaf espresso? A tall-skinny-why bother?"

—Grafitti at the L-Café, Williamsburg, New York

When you visit a coffee bar or café do you tend to order the same drink each time? Below is a list of popular coffee drinks. Find the one(s) that you drink most often and then go to the personality trait list on page 31 to see what your favorite coffee says about you.

::COFFEE BOX: Name Your Drink::

Espresso: A single cup of espresso coffee, drunk black, often with sugar. It should ideally be made from beans ground an instant before being drunk, and it is the base for the drinks below. There's nothing quite like the intense flavor of an espresso. The word espresso is short for café espresso, which means, quite literally, pressed coffee. Espresso has been described as being the very soul of coffee. Deliciously smooth with a rich flavor, a lingering aroma, and a caramel-like sweetness, it is the first choice for many coffee lovers. The term espresso is used to describe both the drink and the apparatus needed to make it, which forces steam through the finely ground coffee beans.

Helpful tip: In general, the more coarsely ground the coffee, the longer it needs to brew. Espresso uses a very fine grind, whereas a cafetiere, or French press, uses a much coarser one.

Double espresso: Twice the size of a single expresso

Cappuccino: One-third espresso, two-thirds hot milk and froth, heated up with steam and sprinkled with chocolate (although a true aficionado would never sprinkle it with chocolate). It should not be too milky to let the flavor of the coffee come through.

Café latte: One part espresso and two or three parts of foamed milk. Milkier tasting than cappuccino. The milk and coffee should be poured into a thick glass at the same time. This drink has largely been popularized by the many American-style coffee shops that have appeared in recent years.

Café au lait/café con leche: Made by topping a shot of espresso with hot milk, usually served in a bowl. This type of coffee is often a European child's introduction to the wonderful world of coffee.

Café corretto: An espresso with a dash of spirit

Café freddo: A shot of sweetened espresso that is cooled by shaking it with ice in a cocktail shaker, then strained into a chilled glass. The coffee will have a fine layer of crema and is usually served at the end of an evening meal.

Café latte freddo: Hot espresso that is mixed with cold milk—the proportions are one-third espresso to two-thirds milk—and shaken with ice. The coffee should be strained into a large glass, but you can serve it with ice and a couple of straws if you prefer.

Espresso Americano: An espresso diluted with hot water, also known as café grande or a long espresso

Espresso Romano: Espresso served with a twist of lemon peel

Espresso corretto: Espresso served with a dash of amaretto or grappa

Espresso macchiato: An espresso served in a small glass or cup (which is what **macchiato** means) marked with a dash of hot milk froth. Despite being a milky coffee, you can drink this after dinner, even in Italy where such things are frowned upon!

Latte macchiato: A large glass of milk with a shot of espresso

Espresso con panna: An espresso with whipped cream

Espresso ristretto: An espresso with less water than usual

Coffee granita: This is a grainy iced coffee. Mix 1¼ cups (300 ml) of freshly made espresso with 1 cup (200 g) of soft brown sugar and 3 tablespoons (50 ml) of brandy, then freeze, stirring every two hours until a light crystal texture is formed. Serve with a spoon as a delicious cool way to end a meal.

Café mocha: A cup of pure indulgence. Espresso shot with chocolate syrup, steamed milk and whipped cream and a light dusting of chocolate.

Drip (filter) coffee: 2 tablespoons of beans to every 6 ounces of water to ensure a pure, satisfying flavor.

Iced coffee: Put ice cubes in a tall, chilled glass. Pour cooled extra-strength freshly made coffee into the glass and serve. For a variation, use coffee ice cubes. Freeze fresh, leftover coffee into ice cubes and use them with regular-strength coffee. For a special treat, a scoop of vanilla, chocolate, or coffee ice cream gives a wonderful contrast in flavor and color.

Has your favorite drink become a habit? Do you think it says something about the kind of person you are?

::COFFEE BOX::
What Your Drink Might Say about You

Espresso: You are smart and sophisticated and give 100 percent all the time. Your idea of a relaxing weekend is to run a marathon or study advanced algebra. You like your life to be organized and are never seen without your organizer—usually a palm pilot.

Cappuccino: You are a bubbly and fun person and the life and soul of the party. You have a tendency to dramatize and love a good gossip, especially over a cappuccino, or two or three.

Café latte: You are comfortable and easygoing—too easygoing sometimes and people take advantage of you. You hate alarm clocks.

Café mocha: You like to look your best. Everybody is your best friend—when you want something. You have charisma and can be a little bit of a temptress or a tease.

Drip (filter) coffee: You are talented and hardworking but rarely get the credit. There is always some "good" reason why you didn't do as well as you could have. You love to talk and seem to know a little about everything.

Iced coffee: You are cool and detached. It's not that you don't want to commit; it's just that life is too exciting and you love your freedom. You have lots of admirers but none that you feel you can open your heart to.

Of course, this is just a game. Espresso drinkers aren't all smart and sophisticated, and not everyone who drinks cappuccino is bubbly and fun. But playing this game can help us think about the roles we play and the images we project to others. Are you somebody who is sincere? Are you a gossip? Are you commitment phobic? Are you a good friend, mother, father, son, daughter, wife, husband, colleague? What does your "look"—your posture, clothes, hair—say to others? What is the first impression you give to others? Are you warm or distant, friendly or moody? Are you pretending to be something you are not? It's easy to get stuck in a particular role. The question is: Is the role you are choosing to create one that makes you happy?

If you want to enjoy your coffee, you need to make sure it is fresh. If you want to enjoy life you need to periodically review and update your self-image. Be honest with yourself. Have you created your experience in a way that works for you? Would challenging old habits—even small ones like the kind of coffee you drink—be a way to freshen up your life?

::COFFEE BOX: Milk and Froth::

When you add milk to an espresso, a new drink is created and the flavor of the coffee changes. Most milky coffees are considered to be breakfast drinks, and in Italy drinking cappuccino after midday is a real no-no.

A French press, or cafetiere, can froth milk beautifully. Warm the milk in a pan to just below boiling point and transfer it to a French press so that the milk is about one-third of the way up, leaving room for the froth to expand. Pump the plunger several times to create your froth. Leftover milk should not be reheated and refrothed. You can also use small battery-operated milk frothers but for the easiest low-tech solution, pour heated milk into a plastic mineral water bottle, close tightly, and shake to create your froth.

:: Don't Face Your Problems Alone

*"Love is when mommy makes coffee for my daddy and she takes
a sip before giving it to him, to make sure the taste is OK."*

—Danny, age 7

We are social creatures and need to discuss our problems with
others, whether it is with those who care about us or with those
who have faced similar difficulties. When you are alone, problems,
disappointments, mistakes, and setbacks seem huge; when you
share them with others, you gain perspective and find solutions.

An experiment was conducted with a group of women suffering from low self-esteem. Some were introduced to women with similar problems, and others were left to work things out on their own.
Those who interacted with others showed a dramatic reduction in
their problems. Those who were left alone showed no improvement. Two heads are better than one. If something is worrying you,
share your problem with someone you trust. Don't keep it to yourself. So what are you waiting for? Invite a friend over for a coffee.

::COFFEE BOX: Coffee Soda::

This is a drink made for sharing. In a tall soda or malt glass com-
bine one cup of brewed coffee with one teaspoon of granulated
sugar. Stir in a third of a cup of half-and-half. Add a large scoop

---

of coffee ice cream and fill the glass to the top with chilled club soda. Add a dollop of whipped cream, dust with some chocolate sprinkles, and top with a cherry. Insert two straws.

:: The Recipe for Success

You'll never make a decent cup of coffee from reused coffee grounds. You'll never find fulfillment in life if you don't leave the past behind. We all like to stay in our comfort zone, where everything is familiar. It's easy and doesn't require too much effort. We feel safe and secure. New things make us feel nervous and uncomfortable. But this territory is the place to go for opportunity.

Taking a risk is always scary at first. Once you realize that you are not going off a cliff and are going to survive, you become wiser and stronger, even if embracing the challenge was a mistake. Don't confuse risk with recklessness. Risk is about calculation and weighing up the odds before you take chances. Reckless behavior is the absence of calculation.

Anything that moves you forward is good, even if it is anger. A "who needs you anyway" or "your loss" attitude can be very positive. On the other hand, anxiety, despondency, and revenge are self-destructive. When you hear the word **no**, don't make rude phone calls, slash clothing, or sit in a depressed stupor. Instead, let rejection motivate you to get right back to work. No isn't the end of the world. It's information, and far better than being left wondering.

If something doesn't go according to plan or a relationship breaks down, tell yourself that no amount of self-pity and tears is going to change the situation or bring your partner back. Cry, swear, kick a punching bag and then stand up and tell yourself you'll be okay. No is bad. No stinks. But at least you know where you stand and can start focusing on what to do next. Think of this loss as a temporary setback, not a permanent problem. To get what you want in life, you must keep moving, generating action, and welcoming new opportunities.

Think of no as meaning, "Not this way; let's look for another, better way." If a diet isn't working, seek advice from a dietitian. If you don't get the promotion, consider other work opportunities. If a business idea is rejected by one person, seek advice from someone else. Don't limit yourself to one way of getting what you want. Be ingenious. Try other approaches—even bold, not-the-way-it-is-usually-done approaches. Just because something has never been done before doesn't mean you shouldn't try. Just because someone says you shouldn't, doesn't mean you can't.

Nothing eases disappointment faster than new challenges. Whatever loss you have suffered, try easing your suffering by welcoming new challenges. Getting involved in a new opportunity will tend to curb the obsessive thinking that may be left over from the loss. And there's nothing like new accomplishments to rebuild whatever self-esteem you may have lost overanalyzing your disappointment. This isn't to say that you should ignore heartache and bury yourself in work. But once you have thought through the problem and you understand why it happened, you should take steps to occupy your mind. Otherwise negative thoughts will return, and you'll start to put yourself down.

Sometimes we have to acknowledge that, despite all our best efforts, we can't have what we want. The man or woman of your dreams turns out to be a nightmare or isn't interested in you, the perfect job opportunity slips out of your hands, you aren't ever going to squeeze into a size ten pair of jeans, and so on. When that happens you need to stop fighting and accept that life isn't going according to plan. But maybe—just maybe—there is a better plan. It is still possible to look ahead and move forward with optimism.

When you hit an obstacle and can't get past it, get curious about what the future holds. Don't think problem, think challenge and opportunity. You never know what could be waiting around the corner. As soon as the cup empties, it can be filled again, perhaps with something better. That's the way the world works.

:: Improve Your Judgment

"The discovery of coffee was, in its way, as important as the invention of the telescope or of the microscope. For coffee has unexpectedly intensified and modified the capacities and activities of the human brain."

—Heinrich Eduard Jacob

To learn from mistakes instead of repeating them, sometimes it is necessary to improve your judgment. Those who stubbornly believe that their approaches are right and everyone else is wrong are often disappointed as a result of their narrow-minded outlook.

Good judgment is all about fashioning your behavior to minimize misfortune. Poor judgment is not being able to assess the repercussions of your actions. Good judgment requires you to ask two fundamental questions: What can I say or do that will help me get what I want? What impact will my actions have on other people?

Unhappy people don't ask themselves these questions. They seem determined to repeat the same action over and over again, whether or not it gets them the result they want.

Good judgment can increase your chances of getting what you are looking for. Learn as much as you can about the issues involved. Listen to as many knowledgeable people as possible before taking action.

Think before you act. Consider possible fallout. Ask yourself these questions:

Do I have to act now?

How will taking more time help?

What do I want to say or do?

Who will be affected?

Who will be offended? Does it matter if they are?

How can I offend the least number of people?

If I can't avoid hurting people, how can I ease the pain?

Put yourself in other people's shoes to anticipate how they will respond. You may decide you need to go ahead regardless of their reactions, but the fact that you have thought about it makes you better prepared and less likely to attract a negative response. If you can learn to see things from another person's perspective before sharing your own, your chances of rejection and disappointment are decreased.

Good judgment involves respecting and valuing other people. So, show other people you care by simply taking time to listen to the feelings, body language, and true meaning of what they say without judging, advising, probing, lecturing, spacing out, pretending to listen, listening for what you want to hear, or seeing things from your point of view only.

Be willing to learn from others. Judgment that is narrow can lead to small-minded actions that are doomed to failure. Minimize your chance of mistakes by being willing to broaden your perspective. Really take in what others say, and be willing to adjust your views when you encounter greater wisdom than your own. If you take the time to listen, your chances of being understood and perhaps getting what you want in life are far greater. With greater listening and a broader perspective comes improved judgment. You choose more wisely, and you demonstrate your ability to learn from your mistakes and not repeat them.

:: A New Perspective

If you think negatively about yourself and keep telling yourself you aren't good enough, smart enough, handsome enough, interesting enough, how can you expect to succeed? No wonder you keep coming across setbacks. The problem is not the reality of your life. It is what you are telling yourself about your life.

Tell yourself right now that you no longer have to live with the interpretations you or other people put on you in the past. You throw away coffee grounds once they have been used, so throw away those negative tapes and be open to the possibility of success. All you have to do is choose to change your perception. You'll be surprised at how easy it becomes to see life from a new perspective.

From now on, base your decisions on the here and now, not on what has happened in the past. Start talking about yourself the right way. Your attitude to life is the key. Never forget one thing: if life gives you a thumbs down, if things aren't going your way, you are still the voice of your life. It is through your voice that **you** will find the strength you need to create success. You can't rely on anyone else's voice, however motivational. Yours is the only perception that can make a difference in your life.

You are also the only person who can teach other people how to treat you. Learn to negotiate with everyone in your life to get the treatment that you need and deserve. Be the one who sets the tone. If people aren't treating you well, think about what you might do to change the situation. Ask and expect the respect you deserve. If someone is physically, mentally, or emotionally abusing you, you did not teach them to do that, and you need to get immediate help or escape from it.

The most important relationship you have—and the one that sets the tone for every other relationship—is the one you have with yourself. People will watch how you treat yourself. Treat yourself with love, respect, and dignity, and you send out a clear message that you are in a position of strength and power. You will gather around yourself people who treat you with respect, and who will reinforce your new perspective.

:: Bounce Back

Terrible things do happen to people, and all of us will face setbacks at some points in our lives. The important question is not "Why is this happening to me?" but "How can I bounce back from adversity?" When things go wrong, we often feel at our lowest, but you have all the skills you need to deal with setbacks. You will survive this if you:

- Accept the reality of what has happened.
- Don't allow your mind to keep replaying the event.
- Imagine yourself coping well and moving on to a new future.
- Don't blame yourself or anyone else for your misfortune: bad things happen.
- Don't compare yourself with anyone else: there is nothing to be gained from it.
- Believe that you are strong and capable and know how to bounce back. Fill your mind with empowering thoughts to help yourself feel stronger and more effective.
- Realize that you will have dark times when you feel that there is no way out, but the darkest hour **is** before the dawn. You will get through this.

We can all look back and regret our actions, but the past is something we can't change. If we continue to agonize over what we should and should not have done, we will remain stuck in the past. Stop blaming yourself or anyone else, let go of guilt, and create a new positive future. Life is full of setbacks, and the only way to survive them is to accept them without bitterness and move forward into a freer future. If you can do this, you will deal with whatever life throws at you, for you are a survivor.

::COFFEE BOX:Fortune in a Coffee Cup::

Those old, used coffee grounds aren't entirely useless. Tea-leaf reading is a well-known method of divination, but diviners in the Middle East look for images in the dregs of their coffee.

When you polish off your morning brew, what do you see? An empty cup streaked with coffee grounds or images of angels, lightning bolts, and pots of gold? The only things you need to read your fortune are a little ground coffee, a clean cup, and lots of imagination. The grounds are already in the coffee no matter whether it it's drip, espresso, pressed, or from the stand in the street. Every cup you drink may hold the secret to your future. Want to try it?

The next time you drink your coffee, think intently about a question you have. When you have drunk the cup, pour any excess coffee that may be left into a saucer, turning your cup clockwise three times.

Now, look into your empty cup. At first, all you will see are streaks of grounds, but look closer. Open your mind. What do you see? Perhaps a ring? Is someone about to get married? How about that cat? Are you keeping a secret? What about that bridge? Are you about to make an important decision?

Practice on your family and friends, and soon you will be able to tell fortunes in minutes. Here are a few symbols that might be seen during a coffee ground reading to get you going; let your imagination do the rest:

Apple or fruit: Creativity

Arrow: If it points up, the answer is yes; if it is sideways, the answer is maybe; if it points down, the answer is no.

Baby: Expect news about the patter of tiny feet.

Brown: Time to make changes in your appearance

Bubbles: A sign of parties and fun

Bugs: A warning to act with caution

Butterfly: A sign of happiness

Cake: The fulfillment of your desires

Camel: Burdens and worries are holding you back.

Camera: Someone is watching you.

Car: A trip lies ahead.

Castle: A sign of isolation and overwork

Cow: You will meet an old friend or former lover.

Coins: Money is on the way.

Cigarette: You have a new plan and need to follow it through.

Clouds: New ideas

Confetti: A good friend is coming to visit, and you will have lots of fun

Cup: Be thankful for what you have.

Cushion: Is life a little too easy?

Desk: Get your papers in order.

Dice: Your fortune is changing—this could be for the better or for the worse.

Dish: Your harsh words could have hurt someone deeply.

Dog: A loyal friend

Drums: Success will be yours.

Envelope: A surprise letter or package

Fire: Passion or lust; great for lovers

Fishes: Wisdom and blessings for you

Flowers: Happiness

Fork: Arguments lie ahead.

Frogs: Great sign of fertility

Hammer: A reliable and confident person

Hat: A sign of secrets

Horseshoe: Good luck

Key: Follow your dreams.

Knots: Try to worry less.

Lips: Love and romance

Monster: You are under stress.

Mouse: You are being taken advantage of.

Necklace: News from an elderly relative

Numbers: Important numbers or dates in your future

Question mark: A question needs to be answered.

Rainbow: Good fortune and happiness

Ring: Marriage—if it is broken, divorce

Road: Travel and adventure lie ahead.

Scissors: False friends

Spider: Success in finance

Stairs: Change for the better

Ship: Major changes lie ahead.

Trees: You are a strong and noble person.

Principle #3

Use the Correct Grind

About Coffee:
Use the correct grind for your coffee maker. If you grind too fine, this will cause bitterness. If your grind is too coarse, the coffee will be watery.

About Life:
Put right what you can, and accept what you cannot.

Choose your responses to situations carefully. Take appropriate action if you can, but if you can't, learn to let go.

:: Life Rewards Action

"In his travels he passed by a coffee bush and nourished himself, as is the custom of the pious on its fruit which he found untouched. He found that it made his brain nimble, promoting wakefulness for the performance of religious duties."

—Najum al-Din al-Ghazzi

So far in this book we have talked a lot about the kind of fulfilling, contented, and successful life you want, but no matter how much you believe in your ability to succeed you still have to get up and do something. Principle #3 urges you to move from being to doing. It is time to take action.

Meaning well isn't good enough. Just hoping for something or having a plan won't make it happen. The only way to get anywhere is take action. You can find success only by walking toward it.

If there is something you've been wanting to do, take action today so you don't miss your window of opportunity. Make a move that will increase your chances of success. Taking action doesn't guarantee a good outcome, but not taking action certainly prevents it. When you act, you will face obstacles, but tell yourself that you will find the strength to work through them. You may be rejected, but tell yourself how important it is to persevere. Remind yourself that you are only a failure if you do not try.

:: Put Right What You Can

Action that is effective needs to be appropriate. If the grind you use for your coffee isn't right, the coffee won't taste good. So, if the action you take isn't appropriate for the situation, the result will be less than you hoped for.

The best approach when facing a challenge is to ask yourself one simple question: "Can I actually do anything about this?" If the answer is yes, then you can start problem solving. Do whatever you can to change the situation for the better. Here are some coffee wisdom tips.

List as many ways as you can of dealing with the situation. At the beginning, you need to give yourself as much choice as possible. The more choice you have, the more chance you have of selecting a method that is right for you. This is also called brainstorming. List as many solutions as you can, even if they seem far-fetched. Suspend your judgment and all the reasons why this or that won't work, and let those ideas come. Later on you can decide whether your goals are realistic and attainable.

When you've listed as many solutions as you can, even the trivial and outrageous ones, it's time to decide what to do. It might be helpful to list all the pros and cons associated with a solution. Make a list of all the good and bad consequences. It will help you clarify the issues and consequences associated with a particular decision. For example, if you can't make up your mind to apply for a job, the pros could be that you get the job, gain interview experience, and so on. The cons could be that you don't get the job and your present employer finds out.

When choosing between options, you need to ask yourself what you really want to happen. Remember that your real needs aren't always easy to recognize. You may want something, but you may also feel that others expect something of you. You may have taken ideas and values on board that don't really reflect who you are. It is important when you make a decision that it reflects what you want and not what others expect of you. If you are always thinking in terms of should and ought, start thinking in terms of what you want or, better still, what is in everybody's best interests, including your own. Are you acting according to your own feelings or someone else's?

Once you become more attuned to your own feelings and what you want, life gets a lot easier. You start doing what you feel is right and not what others feel is right for you. You start considering choices you previously wouldn't have considered.

In very specific and concrete ways, decide what will be done, how it will be done, when it will be done, where it will be done, who is involved, and what your backup plan is if something goes wrong. For instance, you may decide that you do really want to change jobs and you are going to apply for it. You decide not to tell your employer unless you get the job. If possible, rehearse in roleplaying or your imagination your chosen solution. Now, you are ready to move to the final stage: putting your solution into action.

Make sure that you are well prepared, and try out your solution. Whether or not the solution is successful, review it, and see what you can learn from the experience.

If your solution worked, congratulate yourself. You may, for example, be offered the job of your dreams. Perhaps you might like to treat yourself. If you aren't used to treating yourself, think about something you would like and indulge yourself. The important thing is to acknowledge your successes. Also make time to think about why your solution worked and what you can learn about your strengths and weaknesses from it.

If your solution didn't work, don't torture yourself with worry and anxiety. Simply try to understand what happened. Say, you didn't get offered the job you wanted. Perhaps you just didn't have enough experience. Perhaps you didn't take something into account. Perhaps you weren't feeling strong that day; perhaps you misinterpreted something; perhaps you didn't have a backup plan or were not prepared enough.

Whatever conclusion you reach, remind yourself that you have not failed. Congratulate yourself for having had the courage to try. Learn as much as you can from the experience and, with the knowledge that you have gained, select another solution and try again. The more solutions you try, the more you will learn and the better equipped you will be to deal with the situation.

It really isn't the end of the world if your solution didn't work. You can always try another approach or go back to the beginning and define the problem again. Don't be discouraged by setbacks. One setback doesn't mean that you will always fail. It just means that you need to pause and think again. It's impossible to know what will happen in the future. Treat each attempt to solve a problem as if it is the first, however long it takes. Remember, doing is far less frightening than worrying about doing.

:: Create Success, Don't Wait for It

Why is it that for some people success seems easy, while for others nothing seems to go right? According to psychologists what truly sets successful people apart is the way they behave. They don't wait for things to happen; they make them happen. Creating good fortune is a skill and an attitude you can master. So, here are some coffee wisdom tips to help you increase your chances of success and happiness.

Open your mind. Successful people adapt when things don't go according to plan. This doesn't mean that they haven't got conviction; it means that they are open-minded and willing to experiment, make mistakes, and explore new possibilities, however ridiculous or impossible they may seem, in their search for a solution. This shouldn't be too hard for you. Coffee drinkers have a reputation for being open-minded, curious people.

What to do: When something doesn't work out, you don't get the job or the holiday you dreamed of, don't give up. Try looking for similar jobs or alternate vacation ideas. Successful people achieve their goals because they never understand the word **no** to mean anything but "not this way, let's look for another way." Put yourself in luck's path more often by suspending your logical mind and trying something that appears unconventional or risky. Think about your wildest dreams. Then assess how much you are hesitating out of fear and consider what you really have to lose if you don't follow your dreams. Maybe the job, the house, or lover of your dreams is waiting for you to make the first move.

Find out what you want. One of the biggest problems for unsuccessful people is not having a clear idea of what they want in life. Indecision creates inaction, and inaction leads to results that you do not want.

What to do: Ask yourself what you truly want. Think about how you will look, feel, and behave when you have what you want. Naming what you truly want means you can begin to direct your life because you have a goal that is precisely and specifically identified.

Work hard, but make it look easy. Most successful people work hard to achieve their goals. But hard work alone isn't enough—many of us work hard. So what are successful people doing differently? They're working hard but making it look easy. A laid-back approach to life gets people on your side. Why? Because we all have doubts and fears, and someone who controls self-doubt and doesn't give in to fears makes us instinctively feel at ease. We like to be around them, and we like working with them. People who make it look easy invite opportunities their way. Coffee drinkers have an advantage here. Research has shown that coffee drinkers tend to be highly focused individuals but they are also people who know how to relax and unwind.

What to do: The next time you catch yourself complaining, stop and take a deep breath. Ask yourself, "Is it really necessary for me to burden other people with my worries right now?" If you have too much on your plate, ask for help or delegate some of your responsibilities to work colleagues or family members. Work with more ease, and people around you will too.

Develop your intuition. Luck is partly intuition, which is a kind of thinking that guides you when you aren't aware of it. It is a knowledge that seems to come from nowhere, a powerful tool that can help you recognize and achieve the happiness and success you want.

What to do: We'll talk more about intuition in principle #4, but for now, think about what help it can be in guiding you toward good fortune. To get in touch with your intuition, you need quiet time to tune in away from distractions. Take small steps. Try turning off the TV and radio. Let the answering machine take messages. Set the alarm an hour earlier and make time to meditate or just have a cup of coffee and think. Jot down thoughts that you think might be your intuition talking. After a week see if a pattern emerges. Practice using your intuition when the phone rings. Who is that calling? Have fun seeing if you can improve your accuracy rate.

Take your time. How often have you heard people say about meeting that special someone, "I gave up looking, and then he (or she) showed up." Lots of people miss out on good luck because they aren't patient enough to wait for it. They want quick fixes and easy fortune. But sometimes the most important thing you can do to bring good luck into your life is to bide your time. This isn't the same as giving up or being lazy. It is about resting until the moment is right.

What to do:

- **Take a break:** Are you worn out and exhausted? Are you pursuing your goals but not getting anywhere? Are you afraid to stop because you worry you'll never get what you want? If you are, take a break and do something different right now: book a vacation, make plans to see friends, go shopping, read a novel, think about something else.
- **Tell yourself that nothing is so important you have to resolve it now:** Take your time. Have a coffee. Sleep on it. If other people are trying to make you resolve it, let them wait. Give problems time to work themselves out. Wait until you feel detached and at ease and have examined every angle so that you can make good judgments and solid decisions.

Give and receive in equal measure. Quality coffee shouldn't be ground too much or too little. You need to get a happy medium. In life, you need to give and take in equal measure. Successful people tend to be generous people—generous with their time, money, ideas, or resources. When you help other people without expecting or asking for repayment, you double your chances of good luck. Not just because they might help you in return one day, but because the joy created by your generosity will make you feel good about yourself. And when you feel good about yourself you feel more optimistic, which automatically makes life go smoother.

What to do:

- **Begin each day by promising to do at least one thing that will make someone else feel good:** Offer someone a compliment, buy coffee for a friend, bring some flowers to someone, leave a bigger than normal tip when you eat out. If you are working with someone, give that person lots of thanks and credit.
- **Accept loving and generous behavior from others:** Other people have a need to give too. Receiving from others may make you feel vulnerable, but to create luck you need to be receptive and spontaneous.
- **Don't burn your bridges:** Everyone you meet is a potential lifeline. You never know when you might need their help.
- **Don't carry around grudges:** Carrying around grudges leads to stress, anger, and eventually to behavior that can ruin your luck. Avoid people who hurt you, and seek out people who make you feel good. Free yourself from grudges and put your energy into something more positive.
- **Don't talk negatively about others:** Stop talking openly

about people you dislike, and if you must gossip, always cast others in a positive light.

Don't worry, be happy. An upbeat outlook helps you work a little harder and a little smarter to get what you want in life. So, to create success in your life, keep your attention on the successes you've already experienced. What you pay attention to, you get more of. The more you turn your attention to how fortunate you are, the more good fortune you will get. Focusing on the positive will make you feel happier—and happy people are the luckiest people.

What to do:

This attitude of mind is so important that principle #7 is devoted to it. For now:

- **Expect success.** Why do lucky charms work? The luck may not be in the rabbit's foot or the lucky watch or bracelet. These things can bring good luck because you expect that they will.
- **Be grateful for what you have.** Lucky people have goals but they also appreciate what they already have. Be grateful for what you have achieved so far, and focus on what is good about your life. Imagine that you are 95 years old. Looking back, what would you appreciate about your age

now? What would you wish you had taken advantage of—
loving relationships, special gifts, good health? Gratitude and
an optimistic attitude are prerequisites for a lucky, happy
life. Squeeze them out of your present circumstances however you can.

:: The Perfect Blend

"Coffee should be black as hell, strong as death, sweet as love."
—Turkish Proverb

Quality coffee is a matter of chemistry. When you brew coffee you
are trying to extract the perfect percentage of the ground coffee into
the brewed beverage. Too little extraction—too coarse of a grind—
means you don't get your money's worth, and too small a grind
means bitter oils that should have remained in the filter end up in
your cup. To take effective action in life, you need to find the right
chemistry and get the perfect blend. This is when synergy happens.

Synergy is achieved when two or more people work together
to create a better solution than either could alone. It's not my way
or your way, but a better way, a higher way. If you listen to an
orchestra or watch a flock of geese or a winning baseball team,
you perceive synergy—individuals working and blending together
to create something better than they would alone.

Synergy doesn't just happen. It's a process, and you have to help it along. You get there by first defining the problem, understanding the point of view of other people, and sharing your own ideas, then creating new ideas and options. This is where the magic happens. If you get other people involved, you can create new ideas that you might never have thought of alone, and one idea leads to another and another.

Have you ever found that something that seemed unsolvable suddenly seemed solvable when you chatted to a friend over a coffee about it? You share your problem, get your friend's input, and suddenly see things in a new way.

Listening to the points of view of other people and sharing your ideas will eventually lead you to the best solution. Then, all you have to do is go for it.

If you follow the above formula, you'll be amazed at what can happen. But it takes a lot of maturity to get to synergy. You have to be willing to share, to listen to other points of view, and then to find a solution that is positive for everyone.

Think again of that orchestra. All the instruments are playing at once but they aren't competing. Individually, they all make different sounds, yet they blend together to create something wonderful. Think again of your coffee. Individually, the ingredients all have different functions but blend them together, get the grind just right and you have a delicious brew.

:: Coffee's on Me

It's great, isn't it, the feeling you get when you help someone out? Even simple acts of kindness, such as making a coffee for someone else or holding the door open, can make you feel good. Why does it feel good? Simple. Because you are making someone else feel good, and that's the most rewarding feeling.

Life isn't really about competition or getting ahead, yet many of us act as if it were. We forget the principle of synergy and think the pie of success is only so big, and if someone else gets a big slice there is less for us. This is a win-lose attitude. If you have a win-lose attitude to life you are forever trying to get ahead at the expense of other people, always insisting on getting your way without concerning yourself with the feelings of others, and feeling jealous when something good happens to other people. In the end, win-lose always backfires. You could end up winning, but you won't feel very happy, and you won't have many friends.

Others fall into the lose-win trap. Lose-win looks prettier, but it is just as dangerous. It's the doormat approach to life. "Do what you like to me. Wipe your feet on me. Everyone else does." Lose-win is weak. It is easy to get stepped on. It is easy to be the nice guy. It is easy to give in, all in the name of peace. It is easy to set low expectations and to compromise. It is easy to hide your true feelings. For little issues, such as who gets what mug to drink coffee from at the office, lose-win is okay. But when dealing with the important things, you must take a stand. If you don't, no one will respect you and you certainly won't find happiness or fulfillment.

A lose-lose approach to life says, "If I'm going down, you are coming down with me." Misery loves company. War is a good example of lose-lose. Whoever kills the most people wins. Is that really winning?

Now, let's turn our attention to the only approach in life that gets other people on your side and minimizes the risks of disagreement and disappointment: win-win.

Win-win is a belief that everyone can win. It's being strong and accommodating at the same time. It's living by the principle of synergy. You care about other people and want them to do well but you care about yourself too and want to succeed too. Win-win is abundant. You believe there is plenty of success to go around. It's not you or me. It's both of us, all of us. It's not a matter of who gets the biggest slice; there is enough food for everyone.

It sounds simple, but it isn't so easy in real life. How do you do it? How do you feel happy for a friend who has just got a great job and you didn't? How do you find solutions to problems that help everyone? It all begins with you. The first step is to build your self-esteem. If you are insecure and uncertain of what you stand for or believe in, it will be difficult to think win-win. The next step is to stop competing and comparing.

Competition is only healthy when it drives you to improve and become your best. Competition is unhealthy when you tie your self-worth into winning or when you use it as a way to impress others. Use competition as a benchmark to measure yourself, but stop competing over relationships, status, popularity, positions, attention, and the like.

Comparing yourself to others is sure to undermine your happiness. Every person has his or her own path in life with its own obstacles. It does no good at all to switch to someone else's path to see how they are doing. You feel vulnerable, like a reed blown in the wind, feeling inferior one minute and superior the next, confident one moment and intimidated the next. Research shows that comparisons with other people reduce happiness significantly. The only good comparison is comparing yourself against your own potential.

If you are committed to helping others succeed and willing to share recognition and recognize your own needs at the same time, you will not only feel happier, you will become a people magnet. Think about it: doesn't everyone love someone who wants everyone to have a good time? Think about how good it feels when everyone gets a piece of the cake. What a miserable birthday it would be if you ate all your cake and didn't give anyone else a slice!

:: Accept What You Cannot Change

We've talked about taking appropriate action that is of benefit to as many people as possible, including you, to solve a particular problem. If you can do something about what is worrying you, do it. But what if there is nothing you can do?

Worrying and getting stressed won't help. This will only make things worse, stop you getting anything done, stop you from having fun, and even make you feel ill. Here are a few examples of things you can't do anything about:

Anything you did in the past

Something that may happen in the future

Anything someone else is doing or thinking

Natural disasters, accidents

If you are worried about something you did in the past, such as failing a job interview or going through a divorce, you are wasting your energy. We all make mistakes. We say and do things we shouldn't. We fail interviews. We hurt people without meaning to. You can't change what you did. The past is over. You can try to make things better, but if nothing can be done, it is time to let go and move on. Worrying can't change the past.

If you are worrying about the future, likewise, you are wasting your time. You are worrying about things that may never happen. Author Mark Twain once wrote, "My life has been a series of terrible misfortunes, most of which never happened."

The term we use to describe the state of mind that continually rehearses negative possibilities is worry. Worry is the root of all evil. It is closely linked to anxiety. Worry is what you think. Anxiety is what you feel. Are you a habitual worrier? Unless you find a way to manage worry, it tends to get worse and worse. Negative possibilities become magnified out of all proportion. It's great to plan for the future. Take care of your health, be careful about your safety, and apply yourself to get a good job. But worrying without taking any action only makes you feel hopeless.

Remind yourself that you are worrying about things that may never happen or won't happen for a long time. Everybody fears dying, but why waste the time you have now by worrying about it? Natural disasters happen, but not every day, and when they do, people pull together and learn to cope. They are certainly not better prepared by worrying.

You may have heard the saying: "Life is too short to stuff a mushroom." There just isn't time to spend giving your attention to things you can do nothing about. Let go of worries that are beyond your control. If you must worry, worry well, i.e. worry about things you can do something about—and then do them! Taking action will help decrease your anxiety level.

The secret of happiness is letting go of situations that you can't do anything about, living every day to the fullest, and enjoying what you do have. Happy people are not people who are rich and beautiful but people who have learned how to worry well.

:: Take Your Mind Off Things and Put Your Feet Up

If you still find it hard to let go try distracting yourself. People watching while you relax over a cup of coffee is a great way to distract yourself when you feel stressed or tense. Try it. Settle down by a window or sit in a café, and just watch the world go by. Look at the people. Where do you think they are going? What jobs do they have? What are their lives like? It won't be long before you feel calmer and more relaxed.

Another way to deal with unnecessary worry is to change your physical state. If you keep active you are less likely to dwell on what is worrying you. Any activity that uses up adrenaline, such as walking, jogging, and cycling, is beneficial. It's even better if the activity involves a lot of concentration too. Disengage from unnecessary worry the minute you feel it wrapping itself around you. You must do this deliberately. Get up, stretch, walk around, and call a friend. Do not settle into a brooding mood.

How you keep active will depend on your situation. If you are worried about work, a game of tennis might help you unwind in the evening. If you are worried about an interview, a brisk walk up and down the corridor might help. If you are physically restricted, tidying your desk or tapping your fingers may release tension. Other distractions include dancing, cleaning your room, reorganizing your diary, and so on.

You can also try distracting yourself with mental stimulation. Try imagining a scene to take your mind away from worrying thoughts. You could imagine every detail in that scene. It may be a beach on a beautiful island or the peak of a mountain. You can practice mental arithmetic or study people as they go about their daily errands. Other mental tasks include recalling a favorite tune in your head, redesigning a house, or recalling a happy day that you had recently.

Focusing on the task at hand will really help distract you from worry. You could listen to the conversation of people around you or immerse yourself in a good book. If you are cooking just think about what you are doing and not anything else.

Distraction techniques can help, but they come with a warning. They don't work for everyone, and they can be harmful if the distraction becomes avoidance. For example, if you are worried about being overweight, don't distract yourself by shopping for expensive clothes; you'll never face your worry and it doesn't go away. Principle #3 stresses the importance of responding appropriately to situations. If there is nothing you can do about a situation, stop

worrying about it, but if there is something you can do, do it. Take
appropriate action and keep your life moving forward.

::COFFEE BOX: The Proper Grind::

The best way to enjoy your coffee is to grind the beans and then
make your coffee immediately. Grinding releases the essential oils
in the beans that are the natural flavor of the coffee. Beans stay
fresher if kept whole and in an airtight container. Grinding your
beans releases the oils, and the hot water soaks them into the
brewing process. Unfortunately, it also exposes them to their great
enemy, air, which makes coffee become stale.

Today coffee beans are ground with metal millstones using ser-
rated edges. There are a whole range of grinders for home use but
the best are the ones that work on the same principle as the mill-
stone, whether cranked by hand or electric. You can keep out
harmful oxygen by putting the ground coffee in an airtight container in the fridge or freezer. A cold temperature slows down the
rate of oxidation, and an airtight container stops the coffee picking up other aromas—something it is prone to do.

Use the correct grind when you make your coffee. There is only
so much goodness in a given measure of coffee. Grinding too fine

just extracts the bitter-tasting components of the coffee. Ignore anything you hear: no one in the history of coffee making has been able to make more than forty 6-ounce cups of coffee from one pound.

Every coffee maker is designed to brew coffee using a specific grind. In general, the faster the brew cycle, the finer the grind (good for espresso), and the slower the brew cycle, the coarser the grind. A coffee cup is 6 ounces of water poured through 2 tablespoons of coffee, ground correctly for the brewing method.

Use High-Quality Beans and Fresh, Pure, Cold Water

About Coffee:
Use fresh cold water. Water is around 98 percent of every cup; to ensure you get the finest taste, consider using a water filter or bottled water. Choose top-quality beans. For your cup of coffee to be top quality you need to make sure you get the main ingredient right.

About Life:
Celebrate your uniqueness.

Just as the ingredients you use for coffee must be fresh and pure, you need the confidence to be true to yourself and to trust your instincts. Follow every opportunity that allows you to express who you really are, and watch as your creativity transforms you into a deeper, more fully aware person.

:: The Root of All Happiness

> *Coffeepot give us peace*
> *Coffeepot let our children grow*
> *Let our wealth swell*
> *Please protect us from evil*
> *Give us rain and grass*
> —Garri/Oromo Prayer (translated)

The ingredients you choose for your coffee need to be fresh and pure. You were once pure and full of wonder about what life had to offer you—and you can live every day of your life in touch with this sense of wholeness.

See the joy and delight when you look into the eyes of a baby. This was once you—happy with life, trusting, loving, and believing in your own power. You expressed your emotions; you cried when you felt sad or angry: you laughed when you felt happy or excited. You loved yourself. You loved the things you saw. You loved the people who cared for you. You arrived in this world with a sense of self-worth. You believed in you.

When you have confidence and belief in yourself, you feel good. You feel in control of your life and enjoy the challenges it presents you. You feel creative and content, and you make things happen. How often do you feel this good?

As we leave babyhood behind and we start to learn more about the world, we start to doubt ourselves. We find ways to protect ourselves from hurt, and as we lose that trust in ourselves, we lose our confidence. We don't feel so special anymore. It is at this point that all our problems start.

Confidence is the key factor in positive change. Without it no amount of positive thinking, dieting, or meditation will change your life for the better. That's why the fourth principle of coffee wisdom is all about you. It focuses on your uniqueness and your ability to create a strong sense of self, which in turn leads to self-esteem, self-confidence, purpose, and direction. You start making decisions, saying no when you need to, expressing yourself, enjoying your own company. You become the kind of person who is in control of his or her life.

Let principle #4 remind you that self-belief is the root of all happiness. Remember who you are. After all, confidence and happiness are your birthright.

:: Your Self-Image

Your self-image, like the water you choose for your coffee, needs
to be of a certain quality and quantity. If your self-esteem is good,
you will attract success and happiness. If you have a low opinion
of yourself, you will find it hard to attract the kind of people and
opportunities you desire.

::COFFEE BOX: Fresh Water::

Use, fresh, cold water that tastes good. Coffee is 98 percent water,
and if your water tastes bad, your coffee tastes bad. If you use
tap water, let it run for a moment before filling your kettle. If you
don't like the taste of your tap water, experiment with different
bottled waters or filtered waters until you find a taste you enjoy.
And make sure that your coffee-making and -brewing equipment
is clean and fresh too. Coffee contains oil. Every time you brew a
pot some of the residue is left in the container. If the oil in your
coffeepot is not removed, it will affect every pot you brew, making
it taste rancid and bitter.

Water is around 98 percent of a cup of coffee. It is the main ingredient. But like self-esteem it's the most unnoticed ingredient. Your self-image is the most important thing in your life. It guides you in much the same way as an automatic pilot guides an airplane. Until you alter its course, it will keep you going in the same direction. If your self-image is set too low, your life course will head steadily downward. So how can you alter your course to head to the skies?

Start with your conscious mind. Notice when you begin thinking of yourself as a loser. Replace any negative beliefs with more positive images of yourself. For example, every time you think, "I am stupid," contradict this with something positive such as, "I am intelligent."

Just taking a few deep breaths will help you feel more confident. If you feel insecure, a confidence-building technique is to keep telling yourself exactly what you are doing as if you were playing a tape inside your head. If you are at a party, for example, tell yourself, "I'm walking across the floor, I'm looking at people, I'm listening to someone now." It will stop you thinking about how you are feeling. Don't forget, the more you try new things or do things that you fear, the less frightening they become. If nerves do surface, it isn't the end of the world. A bit of adrenaline often sharpens performance, and it sends out signals that you care.

Think about the kind of people you hang out with. Having a

good attitude about those around you is one of the most important predictors of happiness. Whom do you most enjoy having a
coffee with? If you had a challenge ahead of you—whether you
were trying to climb a mountain or trying to meet a deadline at
work—what kind of people would you like to be surrounded with—
people who told you that you would fail or people who gave you
reasons to succeed?

Mix with people who lift you up, and steer clear of those who
drag you down. Success attracts success, just as negativity attracts
negativity. Mix with people you admire, and your self-esteem will
increase too.

Don't give yourself a hard time if you feel insecure and uncertain
at times. Nobody is perfect. There will always be moments when we
feel a crisis of confidence. You can only do the best you can, and if
that is not good enough for others, it's their problem not yours.

Finally, work to change your self-image at a subconscious level.
The most effective way to do this is to learn to use and control
your imagination—a technique sometimes called visualization.

See yourself succeeding. Picture it first in your mind. Believe
you can do something, and then go out and make it happen. You
may ask, isn't visualization just daydreaming or wishful thinking?
No, it is a powerful technique to move you, not in the direction of
your past habits, but in the direction of becoming the person you
want to be.

It may take a few weeks at least before you see any changes, but keep at it. The main thing is to replace negative thoughts about yourself with positive ones, over and over again. Repetition is important. Simply believe and persevere. You are sending data to your subconscious mind that will eventually become your bedrock truths.

As your new self-image grows, you will find yourself becoming more confident and effective. You'll see yourself developing a feeling that nothing the world throws at you can shake you. Other people will start to see in you what you see in yourself. They will react to you differently. You feel better, think better, look better, and become the person you have always wished to be—the confident, successful person of your imagination. As you start to develop this winning side of your personality, you begin to change your ideas about happiness. You don't hope for it, you expect it.

:: Your Unique, Precious Self

Coffee lovers all over the world prize the unique flavor of their chosen beans. Never forget that you are unique.

Consider the incredible lottery that you won at the moment of conception. At that instant a single cell produced by your mother was traveling through her body. Your father, on the other hand, had millions of sperm cells, all of them different. Something or other—fate, chance, luck, God—chose only one of those sperm to fertilize your mother's egg, thus creating the unique being that is you. Had the egg joined with a different sperm cell, the person that is you would never have existed.

There never has and never will be another person on this earth who is just like you. Doesn't that make you feel special and original? Remind yourself every day that you are unique. Enjoy your originality. Whenever you feel the urge to fit in or merge with the crowd pause for a while and think about how special you are. Accept and enjoy your differences. Like the beans that give your coffee its rich and delicious flavor, your differences are what make you a unique and precious person with your own special place in the world.

::COFFEE BOX: The World of Coffee::

The most important aspect of coffee is the unique combination of climate, soil, and geographical position. Coffees vary from country to country, from region to region. Exactly as with wine there are different species of bush and variations in soil and climate. There are, however, a few rules of thumb you can apply:

African coffees (Kenya, Mocha, Tanzania) are spicy and bright with a good level of coffee acidity. Their flavor will hit the tip of your tongue.

South and Central American coffees are smooth and elegant with a hint of nut.

Indonesian coffees are rich and rounded and most exotic with dramatic aromas of hazy tobacco and aromatic spices. They have flavor full enough to support milk and a good balance of acidity.

Mass-market coffees will be blends with the origin often unspecified. Some high-quality coffee is sold under the country of origin but the labeling doesn't tend to be specific. The reason for this is land ownership. Many coffee growers are small farmers who need to join with others to produce enough to sell to coffee brokers.

Coffee Arabica is high-quality coffee from Yemen.

Coffee Robusta comes from the Congo. It is not such good quality but it can be used in blends and to make instant coffee.

Hard beans tend to be the better-quality ones, and the higher the altitude the beans are grown in, the harder the beans are. A coffee expert can tell by sight which beans are hard, but for the consumer the best approach is to ask the retailer and learn by taste.

Each coffee has a different taste depending on its origin. Remember though that the roast determines the strength. Strong coffee is never made by using more coffee—it will just become thick and heavy. The strongest roast is high continental. Light continental is a little milder. French roast and medium roast are lighter still, with mild roast being the mildest.

:: Express(o) Yourself

To celebrate your uniqueness, you must have the courage to express what you really want. If you don't ask for a double shot of espresso, you won't get it. The same applies in life. To avoid tension, misunderstanding, and hidden resentments, be aware of what you need, and ask for it clearly with no hidden agendas.

If this all sounds rather a lot to handle, don't be daunted. Take a sip of your coffee and relax. There's nothing complicated here. Some part of you knows all this already and you just need reminding.

Self-awareness starts by acknowledging that we are all fallible human beings, capable of making mistakes. You are not the only person who gets tense and worried. On the outside others may look calm, but on the inside they may be quivering jelly. When we are self-aware, our confidence is based not on the way we look or on what we have but on accepting ourselves as we are.

When you accept yourself, you feel better about yourself. You learn that not being yourself causes stress and unhappiness. It's rather like getting a weak tea when you have been anticipating a good, strong espresso. Why be the kind of person the waiter ignores? Remember that you have a right to say yes or no on your own behalf. Ask for what you want in a clear and confident way. Have the courage and conviction to stand up for yourself and ask for what you want.

Think about the best kind of conversations over coffee with a friend you have had in the past—how insightful and rewarding they were. The chances are that during these intimate chats you were relaxed, ready to listen, and not on the defensive. You spoke your mind but didn't offer unwanted advice, criticism, and judgment. Try to bring some of those skills to your daily life.

:: Can You Name What You Want?

To bring your unique self to life, it's necessary to know what you want. What makes your heart sing?

If you are lacking in inspiration take a sip of your coffee. It brightens the eyes, quickens the heart, and makes the spirit lighter. Inspiration is just around the corner. Being creative with your life is a divine feeling. Think of an artist who captures the depth of feelings in his or her work. So nurture your creativity no matter what you do with your life. Don't miss out. Being able to express your thoughts, feelings, happiness, and sadness is a magical way to live.

Think about what inspires you. What do you enjoy doing? Remember just as the perfect cup of coffee begins with fresh, pure water and top-quality beans, you need to begin with a clear sense of direction. Perhaps you don't know where you want to go. The following questions will help you get in touch with your creativity, your deeper self:

- If you could spend a day with anyone—famous, not famous, alive or dead from any moment in history—who would it be?
- Imagine a hundred years from now distant relations in the future are trying to piece together their family tree. What would they find out about you?
- If you could choose five of the people in your life to spend six months on a desert island without contact from the outside world, who would they be?
- If you could spend one day a week doing anything that you really wanted what would it be?
- Imagine that you have gone missing while on holiday abroad and a newspaper wants to interview your family, friends, and colleagues about the kind of person you are. What would you like them to say about you?
- Is there something that represents you—a precious stone, an animal, a landscape? Why does it represent you? We all have talents. We just need to find out what they are. If you can't find your talent listed below think about ones not listed. Are you good with numbers? Good with words? Good with people? Good at observing people? Good at sport, singing, dancing, and drawing? Do you like to share? Do you have a good memory? Are you good at organizing things? Are you mechanical? Good with your hands? Do you have flair for fashion? Do you like speaking in public? Are you a good

listener? Do you feel close to animals? Are you a creative thinker? A decision maker?

- Think of a sentence or two that sums you up. It can be a line from a song or poem you know, or it can simply be your own thoughts.
- Thinking about your answers will help you discover your creativity, what your life is about, what is important to you, and what you will and won't neglect to do. It is the roast that brings coffee to life. What brings you to life? Take all the time you need to find out because once you know this it is easier to make sure that each step you take is in the right direction.

::COFFEE BOX: The Roast::

It is the roast that brings the coffee to life. The right roast may add sparkle to a high-quality bean but it can't rescue a mediocre one. By contrast a bad roast can ruin a high-quality bean. Too short and light and it will taste dull, too long and it will taste thin and burned.

The principles of roasting are always the same. The beans are poured into an enclosed preheated container and kept moving so they color evenly. You'll hear the beans pop like a pan full of popcorn. They won't snap open but will open slightly as if they are grinning at you. The noise subsides as they smoke, and then it starts up again. Now, the beans are ready, and the air is filled with the wonderful aroma of fresh coffee. How much longer they are roasted depends on the strength of the roaster. Leave them too long, and the beans will be in flames. An average of 20 percent of the weight of the bean is lost in roasting; that's why cheaper coffees tend to have a toasty flavor—they have not been roasted properly. Mild- and medium-roasted beans are dull colored. It is only high-roast beans that have a delicious sheen from the oils driven out through the roast.

The aroma of roasting coffee has not been without its dangers. In the late 1700s Prussia's Frederick the Great banned the consumption of coffee by ordinary citizens. He wanted his people to drink beer, the drink of his homeland, and he hired retired soldiers to arrest anyone smelling of coffee. He also encouraged doctors to tell patients that coffee drinking caused sterility. Hence Bach, father of twenty children, created his famous musical protest "Coffee Cantata."

:: Where Are You Going?

"I have measured out my life with coffee spoons."

—T. S. Eliot, "The Love Song of J. Alfred Prufrock"

If there is no one like you in the world, then there is no one taking your exact path—and no one will arrive at exactly the same place. So, you have the freedom to choose the path and the goals that are best for you.

How do you choose the goals that are best for you? One way is by planning ahead. Looking ahead is something you do all the time. You write a list of people you want to buy Christmas presents for. You look at your map to plan a long car journey. You make sure that you have the right ingredients before you bake a cake or make a coffee. Planning is a part of life.

Let's do some forward thinking right now. Close your eyes for a few moments and imagine that you are looking into a mirror. The reflection is hazy at first, but the mist soon clears and you start to see yourself. But it is not you today. It is you in ten years' time. What do you look like? What have you done with those ten years? How do you feel?

After a few moments of reflecting on yourself in the future, come back to the here and now. Did you get in touch with yourself? Did you get a feel for what is important to you and what you would like to achieve? This is looking ahead, and it is a great way to turn your dreams into reality.

You may not want to think much about the future. Are you a live-in-the-present, go-with-the-flow type? Living in the moment is terrific, and we'll explore this more in principle #7, but going with the flow that's set by others takes you downhill. You end up doing things that aren't about you at all. You end up nowhere. Don't assume that the herd knows where they are going. They probably don't. The only person who should take the lead in your life, right now, is you.

So at all times strive to be yourself. Drink coffee. Hang out in coffee bars. Mingle with the crowd. Stand out from the crowd. Observe and be observed or just ignore everyone and enjoy your cup. Above all just be yourself. Celebrate your uniqueness and head in the direction that is right for you.

Not being you is a little like drinking instant coffee. Every year the coffee industry invests large amounts of money in pursuit of the ultimate goal—an instant coffee that tastes as good as the real thing. The quality has certainly improved over the years, but an instant coffee will never be able to replace the flavor, body, and aroma of a freshly roasted, freshly made cup of real coffee.

::COFFEE BOX
Instant and Decaffeinated Coffee

Instant coffee requires only a spoon, a cup, and some hot water. Other than convenience, there is not much to recommend it. Most instant coffees are made from poor-quality beans and are brewed in industrialized percolators. The grounds are overextracted, and too much of the aroma and taste disappears. Aromatic oils must then be added back to the granules. The only real advantage to instant coffee is that it is easy to use it in recipes calling for coffee flavoring when no extra liquid is needed. Astronauts also find it handy! It is better to think of instant coffee just as a pleasant, stimulating drink and not something connected with real coffee.

The same applies to decaffeinated coffee. Caffeine is a white alkaloid substance, which is a diuretic and can cause palpitations if taken in large doses. It consists of around 3 percent of the total weight in a coffee bean and is not destroyed by roasting. If you are trying to cut down on caffeine but still want the pleasurable taste of coffee, there are some alternatives. You can drink decaffeinated coffee, which has had the caffeine removed from the beans before roasting. But despite the best efforts of the coffee industry, it is still not possible to extract caffeine without damaging the flavor. High-quality Arabica coffees have about half the caffeine content of poor-quality Robustas, so the first step if you want to reduce your caffeine intake is to drink better-quality coffee. The next step is to limit your intake to two or three cups a day.

The perfect cup of coffee looks tempting and inviting. The next time you are in a coffee shop have a look at the posters or advertisements they have on the wall of their specialty coffees. They look tempting, rich, exciting, and inviting. You want to drink them, to enjoy their unique flavor.

::COFFEE BOX: Cappuccino::

What could be more tempting than the thought of a steaming cappuccino? A shot of the finest espresso with steamed milk and creamy frothed milk with a shake of chocolate.

Handy hint: To make a successful cappuccino the cup must be warm when the milk is poured in or the froth will deflate. That's why in many coffee bars the cups are stored upside down on top of the espresso machine.

Fascinating fact: The drink is called a cappuccino because the topping of frothy milk was thought to look like the large hood or cowl of a Capuchin monk's habit.

Have the courage to be yourself and don't be afraid to let your unique aroma float around the room and into the world. Remember, you are already unique, tempting, and inviting, simply because there is no one else like you. All you need now is a little courage to be yourself.

Try some of the coffee wisdom tips below for natural social success. If you feel that the tips focus on outward show, rest assured that their purpose is always to help the real, genuine you shine through.

Carry yourself with confidence. Lengthen your spine, allow your shoulders to lift, and breathe into your abdomen and chest. Your head will lift and you'll get a new sparkle in your eye. Don't shrink or overprotect your body, because this will look defensive. Keep your hands away from your face when you talk, and try not to fiddle or fidget, because these are sure signs of nervousness. Send out the message that you feel terrific and aren't apologizing for who or what you are.

Always look the part. Dress neatly and colorfully. Every time you dress you send out signals that this is how you are choosing to be. You can opt to wear anonymous clothes that will make you fade in the background, and you can wear baggy, shapeless ones that hide your figure. But if you want to appear confident and charismatic, bold colors such as dark blue, deep red, bright pink, and shiny black will make a more lasting impression.

Do your best to remember names and personal details. Once you get the name-remembering technique under your belt, you'll avoid those embarrassing moments of forgetfulness, which can undercut the charismatic impression you want to create. If you make a mistake, don't try to cover it up. Have the guts to admit it and move on.

Slow down. Avoid the temptation to rush. Take a few deep breaths, and try to calm down. If you rush around, it says to other people that you are not in control of your time. People tend to rush when they feel nervous, so slow your speech, your walk, your movements, and the way you look at other people. Cultivate the red carpet presence. Look calm, gracious and cool. Just glide along. Speak without haste. Fast talkers are enthusiastic, but we associate fast talkers with liars, so slow down and take your time.

See eye to eye. Eye contact says that you are truly interested in the other person and that you are accessible. You may feel self-conscious at first, but this is a skill that can be learned. Look directly into the eyes of the person you are addressing. When the other person has finished talking, look at his or her eyes and wait a few seconds before you answer. This shows that you are engrossed.

A firm handshake leaves a lasting impression. It signifies trust and strength.

Crank your energy levels up. Vitality implies youth and courage and hope—the stuff that dreams are made of. Put your energy into being enthusiastic rather than being focused on your nerves. Enthusiasm is the most contagious emotion you can project. If you convey it to other people, they'll feel enthusiastic too. Enthusiasm gives you a spark. As well as being very attractive, it conveys confidence. It's the key to making yourself attractive to others. So wear your heart on your sleeve.

Try something new. Don't worry about looking stupid. Put yourself in unusual circumstances. This is a great way to build your confidence and learn something about yourself.

Laugh. Projecting warmth is another sign of confidence. It shows you are not scared of other people and that you want to connect with them.

Smile. It's one of the best ways to stick in people's minds. A great smile helps you stand out because it says in the warmest way that you care about the people you meet. It also says that life treats you well, that life is fun, and that you are lucky. A smile can make a huge difference in the amount of good fortune that comes your way. Don't get carried away though. An instant grin carries no weight today. You don't want to be seen as a smiling sycophant. Charismatic people don't flash an immediate smile when they meet someone, as though anyone who walked into your line of sight would do. Instead, they look at the other person's face. Pause. Soak in their persona. Then, let a big, warm smile flood over their face. The split second delay shows that the smile is genuine and only for that person.

Be interested in other people. Lack of confidence is often about being too preoccupied with ourselves. Think of yourself as a researcher. You are finding out what makes the people you are with tick and what their passions are. It helps you become absorbed in others rather than on yourself. The key to charisma is to make other people feel special, and the easiest way to do this is to listen and ask questions. Focus on encouraging other people to open up and feel comfortable with you. Charisma isn't about selling yourself; it is about making other people feel great about themselves. Instead of thinking about yourself when you walk into a room, think about the people in that room. Go and ask how they are feeling, what they are thinking.

:: Their Eyes Met over a Cup of Coffee. (Who Drank It?)

Let's be honest: when it comes to sex appeal, coffee beats tea every time. It's hard to be passionate over a cup of tea—philosophical maybe, but not passionate. Coffee keeps love alive, while tea consoles the brokenhearted. To give spice to your love life, discover the world of coffee and the infinite variety of roasts, grinds, and machines to make your cup of coffee. Is there a special person in your life? Do you want a special person in your life, or are you having fun playing the field? Whether you are looking or not for someone, here are some coffee wisdom relationship tips:

Look your best. Make sure that you always look your best, whether you are going to work or to the dentist or your favorite café. You never know whom you might meet, and first impressions count. Think seductive and smooth, just like the coffee you drink.

Go out and meet people. If you want to meet someone new, you have to get out there and meet them. Find hobbies and interests you enjoy and commit yourself to a gathering of like-minded people.

Ask someone out. If you want a date, you have to make the first move whether you are a man or woman. Smile, make eye contact, and see if there is interest. If you are a woman remember that if you make the first move, he will still think it is his idea!

If you see someone you like, make your presence known fast. Move close enough to talk to him or her and say something that is neutral and polite. For example, if you are at a wedding, you can ask how he or she knows the bride and groom.

Do your homework. Find out what the person you are interested in likes or dislikes, and put yourself in an advantageous position.

Be keen but not too keen.

Don't make the first date dinner. Research shows that dinner is not the best choice. Plan something that involves a little shared anxiety. You could plan to go jogging or walking, riding, or swimming, or to a moving play, a film, or a concert. Then, if it goes well, you can have a coffee afterward to discuss the experience.

Never forget the magic and artistry of love. Like making great coffee, there is a certain amount of alchemy involved. When the moment arrives, listen to your heart. It will know what to do.

:: A New Form of Life

Principle #4 is about building confidence, finding direction, following your heart, and winning the hearts of others. Above all, though, it is about being you. Fresh water has no impurities. It is clear and refreshing. High-quality beans are packed with their own unique flavor. Bring some of those qualities into your life. If you want to find happiness, you need to be true to yourself. You need to follow your instincts. That means working with your intuition.

Whatever you call it—hunch, vibes, insight, instinct, foreboding, revelation, or inner voice—there is a little-used but powerful tool at your command that can improve your chances of success and happiness. It is your own untapped and often overlooked but highly effective intuitive system.

You can't explain why, but you just have this gut feeling. This familiar feeling, if used wisely, can influence your luck. Do you ever have hunches that something is going to happen and more often than not these hunches turn out to be correct? That's your intuition at work.

What do we mean by intuition? **Webster's Dictionary** defines it as the act by which the mind perceives the truth about things immediately and without reasoning or deduction.

Intuition is knowing something without being aware of how you know it. It is an insight that seems to come from nowhere, a sudden knowledge without any logical evidence. Intuition can be heard as a voice in your head. Or it can be a feeling that you need to take it easy or press ahead even if you are afraid. It leaves you feeling that you just know something even though you don't know why you know and there is no rational explanation. It can be soft and gentle, or it can give you a very strong message. Some people think of intuition as their God speaking to them or the wise part of themselves directing them.

It's clear that intuition plays an important role in success. If we could all know what was the right thing to do in the future, of course, our luck would change. Imagine how fabulous it would be to play and win at the stock market time and time again! We all wish we could have such powers. But is it really possible to develop intuition to a degree that it can be used for guidance in practical matters in everyday life? Can it be used to create success? Psychologists believe that it can.

Many artists, writers, painters, and inventors depend on the power of their intuition to amaze the world with their brilliant innovations. Thomas Edison firmly believed that some of his great inventions came from an idea outside himself. When struggling with a problem, he would consider all the angles and then put the matter aside. Sooner or later a flash of insight would give him the solution.

Some people are more intuitive than others and receive flashes of insight frequently, while others experience them rarely. There is, however, growing evidence that most of us possess this ability to some degree. For example, our subconscious mind often tries to warn us when we are in danger. In a split second, an impulse tells us to do something—run, fight, hide, look up, duck—and in many cases this impulse saves our life.

Sometimes we wish our intuition would tell us what to do, but intuitive powers can't be switched on and off, and any attempt to try to do this is futile. Hunches flash into our unconscious unbidden, often coming in the form of an inner awareness or a definite idea of what we should do, gently nudging us in the right direction.

One thing we do know, though, is that intuition tends to come to us when we are in a relaxed state of mind. Sometimes a walk, a good night's sleep, fun times with the family, and, of course, relaxing over coffee are all that is needed for a new form of life to present itself.

:: Instant Illumination

Ever remember thinking, "It's right on the tip of my tongue," but you can't quite remember what it is? Later, seemingly from nowhere, the name or the thought arrives. Here, you have a classic example of your intuition working.

When you are struggling with a problem try this:
Gather all the information you can about the problem. Then concentrate intensely on all the possible angles. Really work at trying to find the best solution and turn the matter over and over in your mind.

Then let go. Completely stop thinking about it. Turn your attention to something else. Enjoy a cup of coffee. Tidy your desk. Take the day off. The problem will slip into your subconscious mind, where it will be processed and filed away. It is now that your intuition gets to work scanning all the information you have stored and making new connections. Then, right out of the blue, a solution will present itself.

A good time to let your intuition solve your problem is while you are asleep. If you happen to wake in the night, make sure that you have a pen and paper handy to write down your solution. After you go to bed, focus on the problem, considering all angles. Limit yourself to thinking about one thing as you lie down to sleep. If other thoughts start to intrude, guide them back to that one subject. Too many thoughts are unsettling and make it harder for us to fall asleep by putting us on edge. At this time just before sleep, your subconscious mind is at its peak receptivity. While you are asleep it will scan your data banks for a solution.

The answer may pop into your mind during the night or in the morning, or it may take longer. Remember, you can't force the process. Don't be discouraged. Keep repeating the technique, and sooner or later when you are relaxed and thinking about something else the answer will come into your mind. Do you doubt that this process works? Then, just try it and see.

If your life is busy, stressful, and cluttered with constant to-dos, the distractions may be too loud for your intuition to be heard. Sometimes, to compete with these distractions, your intuition will get louder and louder, and you may not like what it has to say. For example, if you ignore warnings to take care of yourself, your body may revolt and slow you down by force with a bout of sickness.

Some people find that daily meditation helps, or yoga or tai chi or other activities designed to calm your mind. Take some quiet time for yourself away from distractions, such as TV, radio, and noisy children, and use it to think, imagine, and dream. Set aside time each day for a break of some kind. Your coffee break is the ideal time. Tuning into your thoughts for just ten or fifteen minutes while you relax and enjoy your coffee can make all the difference in helping you connect to your intuitive powers.

If you really want to find what is right for you, your intuition will provide you with the answers, so focus on what you want. Don't let your logical mind come up with all the answers, and don't try to force the process. Instead, be patient and use your intuition gradually and carefully. As you start listening to those hunches, an amazing thing will start to happen: your life will change for the better.

:: Coffee Wisdom Tips to Help Develop Your Intuition

Every time you enjoy your coffee just let your worries and fears melt away. Watch the steam rising. See how the froth bubbles. When you have finished your coffee, take with you that laid-back feeling. Then, when you least expect it flashes of illumination will come.

Sit by a window with your coffee and gaze at the sky and the slow-moving clouds. This can create a restful atmosphere that helps intuition to surface. If you are a passenger in a car or a train, look out of the window at the passing scene. Allow your unconscious tension to fall away. Focus on your breathing, relax, and permit random thoughts to float through your mind. Defer all judgments of the thoughts. The drone of the motor or the crank of the train's wheels can serve as soothing background noise while you permit your intuition to dominate.

Ease gently into a hot bath until you are submerged except for your face. Allow all directed thought to leave your mind. Close your eyes and listen as your intuition takes center stage. Or try gazing at the seashore. Listen to the lapping of the waves. Breathe for deep relaxation with your eyes open or closed. Try to get a feeling for the infinity of life as encompassed in the eternal motion of the sea. Some people become mesmerized watching the rhythmic movement of the waves. In this state of peaceful observation, your intuition has an opportunity to be heard. Or you could listen to music. Listening to our favorite music can help us feel more relaxed, happy, and in touch with our intuition.

The most favorable conditions for receiving intuitive messages are during periods of quiet and serenity when logic is subdued or shut down. This is what happens when you relax with a coffee. It can also happen when you sleep.

Your intuition may come to you clearly first thing in the morning, or it may come to you in a dream with symbolic and metaphoric undertones. Keep a notebook and start recording your dreams, and you may notice a connection between animals, people, or events that crop up in your dreams and decisions you are trying to make. Don't worry about books that claim to interpret dreams. What matters is how **you** interpret the images. What is your intuition trying to communicate to you through your subconscious mind? Watch for puns and allegories; the subconscious mind has a sense of humor too. Seeing a cat may remind you of independence. A cup of coffee may remind you of comfort and happiness. Finding a penny may make you feel reassured if pennies have special significance in your life. It is the significance you give things that matters and the confidence they give you to move forward beyond fear.

You may physically manifest a message from your intuition. Some people always get headaches when they are stressed out. You may hear certain expressions or recommendations several times, and this may lead you to act on them. Or things that have a special significance to you, such as a certain piece of music or a special food, may come into your life at times you need to feel supported, giving you peace of mind and courage. Your intuition may also speak to you in sections—a little bit now, a little bit more a few days later. It is only when you have all the pieces of the puzzle that things start to become clear.

When you know something intuitively, you just quietly know it.

The feeling is much different from the noisiness of fear with its explanations that clatter around in your head. Intuition is also a lot gentler than fear. If the thoughts in your mind are full of shame, anxiety and judgment, they are likely to originate from your conscious mind. Intuition tends to be warmer, gentler, kinder, and nonjudgmental. If the voices in your head say you are a loser, you always quit, you can't do what it takes, then your intuition probably isn't talking. Your intuition might tell you that something doesn't feel right, this isn't the right thing for you, and it's time to move on and change direction and find what works better for you. There may be no words at all, just a gut feeling that it is time to make a change.

If you still aren't sure how your intuition speaks to you, carry a pen and paper around with you and jot down thoughts that come to you randomly that you think could be your intuition talking. They don't have to be earth shattering, just simple thoughts that come to you out of the blue when you are walking to shops, drinking your coffee, or cooking dinner. Don't make any judgments or decisions; just write the thoughts down. At the end of the day, review what you have written and see if a pattern emerges.

:: Believe in Miracles

Something must always be left to chance in life. However hard you try, the water you use for your coffee won't be 100 percent pure, and the coffee you drink won't be 100 percent perfect. If everything could be perfect and nothing unexpected ever happened, the world would be the dullest place that could possibly be conceived. We are all at the mercy of circumstances beyond our control. There will always be things that happen in life we can't understand or explain. Since we will never really know, why not believe that the universe is really a magical place?

Think about the power and magic of luck. Life would be lackluster indeed without the unexpected—the chance meeting, the lifesaving encounter, the lost object that suddenly reappears, those flashes of intuition that tell you something and that then happens—the seeming work of an unseen power.

We have come full circle with coffee wisdom principle #4. We started by saying believe in yourself and your future. We end by saying trust your instincts to take you where you want to go, but don't expect everything to go exactly as you planned. Sometimes good or bad things happen, and we can't explain why. All we can do is respond appropriately, turn the situation to our advantage, try again, and believe that miracles can happen.

Your are living proof that miracles can happen. There never has been and never will be anyone just like you. You are already exceptional and unique. Instead of envying others for what they are and what they have, a state of mind that only leads to debilitating inactivity and destructive negativity, rejoice in what you are, in what you have, and what you can be. Celebrate your uniqueness.

Principle #5

Get the Proportions Right

About Coffee:

The proportion of coffee to water is vital. Experts recommend using 2 tablespoons (10 grams) of ground coffee for each 6 fluid ounces (180 ml) of water. Regardless of how much coffee you make, you need to keep these proportions consistent. Proportions can be adjusted according to taste, but using less coffee makes for a thin, bitter-tasting brew.

About Life:

Challenge irrational thinking.

Keep a sense of proportion and perspective. Life isn't easy, and you may make mistakes, but you are still a worthwhile human being. Challenge negative thinking, and find the discipline to solve problems instead of complaining about them.

:: Life Isn't Easy

"I have tried to show the café as a place where one can go mad."
—Vincent Van Gogh

Principle #5 focuses on the importance of proportion and perspective. To create a refreshing cup of coffee, you need the right proportion of coffee to water. It's the same in life. For a fulfilling, stimulating life you need to keep a sense of perspective. Good and beautiful things happen in life but so do tough times.

Life isn't always easy. Once you know that tough times are normal—once you can understand and accept it—life starts to get easier. Because once you stop trying to avoid challenges and disappointments, the fact that life isn't easy doesn't matter anymore.

Most of us deep down believe that life should be easy, and we complain about our problems. Think about how many times today a little voice inside you has moaned, "Why me, why now, why this? This isn't fair; I shouldn't have to do this!" It's as if we expect our lives to be problem free, but the problem-free life has about as much flavor as watery coffee.

Life isn't easy. Accept that and then decide if you want to complain about your problems or solve them. If you want to keep complaining about them, put this book down. If you want to do something about them, read on.

Only in meeting and solving our problems does life have any meaning. Problems require us to be creative, disciplined, skillful, hardworking, courageous, and wise. Confronting problems helps us grow spiritually, emotionally, and mentally. For all these reasons, instead of dreading problems, we would do well to welcome them.

Most of us can't make this big step. We do all we can to avoid pain. We hesitate, we avoid, we make excuses, we ignore or forget our problems and hope that they will go away, or we deaden ourselves to the pain through addiction or pleasure seeking. We do all we can to avoid our problems rather than deal with them. Trouble is, all our avoidance tactics end up causing more suffering than the problems we are trying to avoid. When we don't face our pain, we stop growing as human beings. We become bitter and stuck. Our spirits begin to die.

As hard as it seems, there is no escaping the fact that problems, pain, and suffering are a part of life. They add flavor to life so that it is rich and full-bodied—not bland and colorless. We all need to find the courage to face our problems, however painful, deal with them, and move on. This is the only way to achieve serenity and fullness in life.

::COFFEE BOX: Café Lingo::

Single: One shot of espresso

Double: Two shots of espresso

Skinny: Made with nonfat or skimmed milk

Short: Small cup

Tall: Medium cup

Grande: Large cup

Vente: Huge cup

Dry: No liquid milk, just foam

Wet: Cappuccino with small amount of milk as well as foam

To go or with wings: To take away

No fun: Decaffeinated

:: Courage

Courage is the power or quality that we need when facing tough times. Are you going through a difficult time right now? Do you feel as if you are stretched to the limit?

Well, now is the time to sit down, have a cry, a cup of coffee—or both—and understand that you will find your courage. Remember principle #5 is about balance and perspective. Just as we all feel fear, each one of us is also filled with the ability to be courageous. All we need to do is connect with the universal energy that surrounds and protects us. It won't make us invincible but it will help us face our fear with an inner strength that is always there if we look for it. Take a deep breath and go inside and find your courage waiting for you. It will give you the strength to carry on.

Perhaps right now you need to have the courage of your convictions. To do what you know is right for you. Perhaps right now you need a sense of discipline and responsibility.

Discipline is the courage to persevere in the face of long odds. The courage to keep your eyes on what you really want—which may take a long time to get—instead of caving in to short-term setbacks. The courage to act in accordance with your own beliefs. To stand up and be counted.

Along with discipline comes a sense of responsibility. Often responsibility is seen as boring and dull. It is associated with restriction, lack of choice, and financial ties. Is that how you see responsibility? If you do, the next time you stop and put your feet up for a coffee break use this time to think again about the true nature of responsibility and the value it can bring.

"Response"-"ability" is the **ability** to **respond** appropriately to any situation you are faced with and to recognize that what you do is your own choice. It means to act with care, thoughtfulness, and respect; to be trustworthy; and to be willing to account for your actions. To be responsible is to be adult in the truest, most fulfilling way.

The greatest responsibility you will ever have is to yourself. You are responsible for listening to your own feelings and making sure that your behavior is always honest and compassionate towards yourself and others. To be responsible is to keep a sense of balance, proportion, and perspective and to choose for yourself the path you will take in life. Begin today.

:: Don't Grind Yourself Down

Don't grind yourself down with negative thinking. It's okay to have weaknesses—to be unpredictable, to make mistakes, to have room for improvement, to jump to conclusions, to misunderstand, and do all the things that make us human. In principle #3, we talked about using the correct grind of the bean. Here, we're talking about keeping a sense of proportion and perspective. Don't let the notion of perfection get in the way for you.

When something is perfect, this means that there is no room for improvement. It is faultless. Think of a perfect square or a perfect right angle or a perfect circle. A perfect circle is 360 degrees—not 359 or 361. The trouble is we try to transfer this mathematical image of perfection on to our lives, other people, and even things, such as the houses we buy or the coffee we drink. In our daily life, there is no exact formula for what is perfect and right. We are not statistics or geometry.

In human terms, perfection is about being imperfect. Think about the people you admire. Do you admire them because they are perfect or because they have beaten the odds, overcome weaknesses, put the past behind them, or are simply doing the best that they can? We aren't robots or comic book heroes without human flaws and emotions. Life is about balance. If we achieve perfection in one area, there are always compromises in others. Relationships may suffer when career goals are achieved. Careers may suffer when family and friends are put first.

Think about where you got your notion of perfection. Real life isn't like our dreams or the magazines or movies, and that is what makes it so wonderful and exciting. If life were perfect, how would we grow? How could we appreciate what was good if we didn't experience its opposite? Doesn't a cup of instant coffee make you appreciate real coffee more?

If you are trying hard to be perfect and control everything in your life, maybe it's time to relax and have the courage to face your feelings. Life is not in our control, only our responses to it are. Kick off your shoes, put your feet up, and reach for that perfectly brewed Java. Because, let's face it, your coffee may be the only thing in life that is possible to get (almost) perfect.

Your life is already perfectly imperfect. Enjoy it for the rich and wonderful experience it is.

:: Challenge Thinking Errors

To keep a sense of proportion and balance, it's important to challenge negative thinking whenever it crops up. The way you think affects the way you feel. If you think you aren't worthwhile or that you can't cope, then you won't feel worthwhile or be able to cope. Becoming aware of how your thoughts are affecting you is a big step forward.

Psychologists refer to unhelpful thinking patterns as "thinking errors." Under stress, you may find yourself making thinking errors such as: thinking in all or nothing terms—one mistake and you are a failure; seeing only the negative in a situation; blaming yourself for everything; losing perspective and blowing things out of proportion—it isn't a mistake, it's a disaster; telling yourself you can't cope; and so on. Indulge these thinking errors for long enough, and you may not even be aware that other thoughts are possible.

You don't have to replace negative thoughts with positive ones, simply with more appropriate ones. Positive thinking can be as unhelpful and as unrealistic as negative thinking. Always looking on the bright side when things are clearly falling apart all around you won't do you any good at all. Negative thoughts simply need to be replaced with more realistic ones. Fortunately, realistic thoughts are more optimistic than negative ones. Realistic thoughts take into account the negative, but they also take into account other possibilities. For example, saying to yourself: "I'm no good at anything" can be replaced by, "There are things I'm not good at, but there are also things I'm good at."

When negative thoughts start to appear, evaluate them carefully. Don't treat them as facts just because you are thinking them. Question them. The trick is to recognize when you have a negative thought and to ask yourself, "Am I being realistic here?" Then, you can move toward replacing it with something more positive. Don't believe everything you think. You don't always believe what other people tell you or what you read in the papers, so why accept everything your thoughts tell you? It's incredible how much freedom becomes available when we start to challenge our own negative thinking.

:: Buy Yourself a Coffee

"Coffee which makes the politician wise. And see through all things with half-shut eyes."

—Alexander Pope, "The Rape of the Lock"

To keep a sense of balance and perspective, especially through tough times, take time out regularly to be kind to yourself. Kindness starts at home; we can only be as kind to others as we are kind to ourselves. Reflect on your achievements, the progress you have made so far, and other positive qualities.

So practice up. Take yourself out for a cup of coffee. Become your own best friend. Imagine that you are having a chat with yourself over a cup of coffee. What would you say that would be reassuring and comforting? How would you encourage yourself to become more confident? What would you say to your friend? Would you give her a hug? Would you tell her that she is doing okay and you appreciate how hard things are but you think she is terrific and coping really well?

When you feel low, become your own best friend and see how much better you can feel about yourself.

When you think about yourself, what kind of person do you see? Many of us are very critical of ourselves, but most of our negative beliefs have no foundation in reality. Changing negative beliefs about yourself will instantly give you more confidence in your abilities. You change your negative beliefs by training your mind to believe positive things instead. Instead of saying, "I am stupid," tell yourself that even though you sometimes do stupid things—as everyone does—this does not make you a stupid person.

Start to appreciate things about yourself, however small they may be. Appreciate your eyebrows, the way you smile, the way you talk. Begin to admire something about yourself, and you will soon find other positive qualities to appreciate as well. You'll find that as you start to appreciate yourself and treat yourself better, your self-image will improve and so will your chances of happiness.

:: Reason, Realism, and Facts

Principle #5 teaches us about the importance of perspective. We may not be able to avoid negative thinking—everybody feels insecure and inadequate at times—but what we can do is balance negative thoughts with more constructive ones. From now on every time you have negative thoughts about yourself start challenging them with realism, reason, and facts. Here are a few tips for dealing with common negative thoughts:

Exaggerating: Do you make mountains out of molehills so that a small setback becomes a major disaster? Does "I totally messed that up" refer to a minor mistake; is a minor cold a near-death experience? Try to get into the habit of describing situations as they are and not dramatizing them. This will help you feel more in control. Okay, you made a mistake, but this isn't the end of the world.

I've failed again: Rather than labeling your mistakes or disappointments as failures, try viewing them as setbacks or learning experiences. This is less final than failure. Think in terms of temporary setbacks, which add to your store of knowledge, whenever you feel disappointed or let down. That way you will feel less inclined to give up and be more willing to try again.

All or nothing: You may think, what's the point of trying, if I'm never going to be 100 percent right or the best at what I do? The point is that there are a lot of advantages to learning new skills. There are great rewards in getting better and better. If you aren't perfect at something, you can still do it well and get lots of satisfaction from it.

That's it, I can't do it: Negative thinkers often tend to believe that if something has gone wrong once it will always go wrong. For example, you have one argument with your partner and decide that the relationship is in crisis. Sometimes when you buy a new gadget, for example a DVD player or PlayStation®, it takes a while to understand how everything works. You keep fiddling and experimenting until you get the hang of it. Persistent effort pays off. Just because you didn't get things right the first time doesn't mean that you never will.

It's my fault: It is impossible for you to be in control of all the factors that create a situation. If you have a tendency to blame yourself when things go wrong, closely examine the circumstances that led to the setback. Some of these may have had nothing to do with you. If something unfortunate does happen, get out of the habit of saying it's your fault because you aren't good enough. You may make mistakes, but you are still a worthwhile human being. Try to replace blaming thoughts with encouraging ones: "This didn't work out, but how was I to know this or that would happen?"

Pessimistic fortune-telling: Nobody can tell what the future holds. Things may turn out bad, but they may also turn out right. Start allowing yourself to see the possibility that things just might work out. Get rid of over-the-top pessimism. If you have a tendency to think the worst of yourself and other people, take a deep breath and think about the evidence for and against your forecast. Start replacing negative assumptions with more realistic ones: "I keep thinking I'll never do well, but how can I tell what will happen in the future?" If you think you'll never amount to anything, repeatedly ask yourself, "How do I know?"

Ignoring the positive: Challenge negative thoughts as much as you can by looking for facts to disprove them. You will start to learn that negative thinking not only makes you feel unhappy, it is also misleading and inaccurate. For every negative thought there is always a positive one. Keep your sense of perspective and balance, and you keep your cool.

:: Keep Your Cool

Add too much or too little water, and you ruin your cup of coffee. Once again, we return to the theme of principle #5: keeping a sense of proportion. We've seen how important it is to balance negative thinking with positive but what about our feelings? Expressing your emotions appropriately and responding sensitively to others is vital for a fulfilling life. How many times have you said things like: I don't know what I feel? I don't know what came over me? I couldn't stop myself?

Having feelings that make you act in a way you don't like is damaging to your sense of self-worth. If you can manage your feelings, you will find it easier to make decisions and see the opportunities rather than the problems that come into your life. If your feelings are getting in the way of doing what you want or being the kind of person you want to be, it is time to take positive action. Completely unshakable emotional confidence is an impossible ideal but there are things you can do to help it become rock solid.

You may find it hard to understand or trust your emotions, yet the very nature of emotions is to be illogical. Sometimes, you just feel sad. Instead of questioning or denying this, simply allow yourself to feel sad. It's not a crime. Feelings, even the so-called negative ones, such as anger, fear, and sadness, are there to be felt. Acknowledge them. Feel them. When emotions are not felt, they cause even greater stress. Emotions are messages that come from your inner wisdom. If they are not worked through in a positive way, the biochemical effect may be physical and emotional tension.

Emotions are the only real way we have to show what matters to us and what doesn't. Difficult emotions signal the need for some kind of change in our lives. They require us to act, to change the situation or mindset that is causing distress, to move forward with our lives. Negative emotions are not bad emotions. They are necessary for us to grow and develop.

Reconnecting with your emotions won't be easy if you are used to denying or suppressing them, but, for a balanced life, it is important that you do start to become more aware of what you are feeling. Once you can do this, it is time to try and deal with them.

Sometimes, you won't know why you are feeling the way you do, and even the thought of your favorite coffee can't cheer you up. There may also be times when what you feel is confusion—you aren't sure what you are feeling. Emotional confusion may cause you to react inappropriately in certain situations. It could be caused by unresolved hurts from the past leaking into the present. If this is the case, recognize that you may not be able to heal every emotional wound from the past but you can choose how much such wounds will control your present. Don't let that hurt undermine your confidence anymore.

The first step in managing your emotions is to accept what you are feeling, try to understand that feeling, and take responsibility for it, even if it is troublesome. For example, if you feel sad, don't blame other people or try to deny that you are feeling low. The next step is to choose how you respond to that emotion. You may use a strategy to induce a state of calm within yourself so that when you act you are acting out of your whole self rather than just out of emotion. For instance, sometimes when you feel sad it helps to have good cry or talk to a friend or just spend time alone.

You can find positive ways to manage the unruly feelings that overwhelm and confuse you. For example, sadness can indicate that you need to change some aspect of your life. Guilt can encourage you to be more realistic about your responsibilities. Shame can encourage you to focus on your strengths not your weaknesses. Anger helps you focus on what is important to you. Jealousy and envy can highlight what you really want for yourself in life. Apathy suggests the need for more mental and physical stimulation. Fear can encourage you to face your problems rather than avoiding them.

Principle #5 teaches us that a full life is about staying balanced, with a sense of proportion about the things that happen. Life will always include both love and hate, joy and sadness, pleasure and pain. That's the beauty, magic, and wonder of it.

:: Keep Your Eyes Wide Open

When you are faced with something difficult, sad, or demanding, it is tempting to look for a shortcut, a way out or a way around. You don't want to have painful or uncomfortable feelings, dwell on difficult events, or do things that are unpleasant.

But as principle #5 teaches us, shortcuts and avoidance tactics never work. Adding too much water won't help you get your money's worth out of your coffee. You just end up with a bad-tasting cup of coffee. It's the same in life. Shortcuts lead us back to where we started from or to somewhere even worse. Your progress will be blocked until you open your eyes, face the challenge, accept the experience, and go through it.

So go through the experience with eyes wide open even if you don't know where it will lead. Face up to what needs to be faced, accept what needs to be accepted, and see things through that you are committed to. Keep putting one foot in front of the other, and you will emerge on the other side, stronger and wiser, with the pain and problem you faced behind you. You will have gained vital understanding and awareness that will be of lasting value to you.

Understand that whatever you are facing, it came into your life to bring you valuable experiences. It will teach you valuable things you need to know on the next stage of your life's journey. Don't resist or fight it. Stop trying to carry on while avoiding it, for if you do this, you'll just create more pain for yourself.

Instead, trust that no matter how hard it feels right now, you can get through this and it will come to an end. Follow the darkness until the light appears. There is resolution and happiness ahead for you, so keep going forward. Challenge negativity at every opportunity. Maintain a sense of perspective, keep your eyes and your heart open. You will be okay.

Principle #6

Boiling Destroys the Flavor

About Coffee:
Boiling causes bitterness, so never boil coffee. It should be brewed between 195°F and 205°F (90°C—96°C).

About Life:
Check your stress levels. Balance your body, mind, and spirit.

If coffee is overheated, it tastes bitter and unpleasant. It is crucial to get the brewing temperature right. Take a look at your own life. Are there times when you feel you are boiling over with stress and tension? If you want to lead a happy contented life, there is no better place to pause and reflect than that indicated in the sixth principle of coffee wisdom.

:: Boiling Point

"Sleep? Isn't that some inadequate substitute for caffeine?"

—Rave

We live in a bustling world of stress. Every aspect of our lives, from our homes to our relationships, our work, our children, our sex lives, and our traveling is a potential hotbed of stress. Even simple pleasures, such as getting a decent coffee when the line at the café seems endless, can at times be stressful.

There is another problem with stress—it's contagious. If a boss is irritable and worried, this rubs off on the staff. If mom or dad is stressed out, the whole family suffers. If the waitress or sales clerk is anxious and unhappy, this can put you off your food or your shopping.

Just the other day I was sitting in my favorite café when a couple sat down at the table beside me. It was obvious that all was not well. The woman snapped whenever the man tried to make conversation and then the accusations started. Within minutes, I along with the other people in the café, had become tense and overwrought in their presence. We were quietly relieved when they finally left. Proof, if any were needed, that stress is infectious.

Sure signs of stress include a dry mouth, clammy hands, skin problems, insomnia, mood swings, loss of libido, and general poor health. Many of us have got so used to feeling stressed that we accept less than perfect health as the norm, but it isn't the norm to feel irritable, ill, and tired most of the time. Starting today, each time you feel stressed, think about that coffee boiling away, becoming more and more bitter.

It is time to stop, turn the heat down, and reflect. What does your life mean to you? Why feel bad when you feel good? Why go against the flow of life? Just press the pause button for a few moments. Take the time to discover a wonderful new perspective.

:: Stop, Cool Down, and Reflect

"At this time to refuse or neglect to give coffee to their wives was a legitimate cause for divorce among the Turks."

—William H. Ukers

So far in this book we've talked about how to deal with tough times, how to take responsibility, and how to be disciplined. Now, it's time to put what we've learned into practice—by stopping to take care of ourselves and manage stress.

If you want a stress-free life, you may as well start looking for a coffin. We need a little stress to keep us on our toes, but too much stress isn't good; it's a sign that we need to change some aspect of our lives.

One of the most terrible things about being stressed is that you lose not only your perspective but also your common sense. You drink way too much coffee to keep yourself going. You phone the psychic line, get your horoscope read again, spend money you haven't got, or make decisions you regret later. In dealing with stress, the most important thing is finding out where there is an imbalance in your life. Forget special diets, expensive retreats, and tranquilizers, finding a balance in your life between work, rest, and play is truly the most effective treatment for stress you will find.

Carefully looking at your life may be all that you need to do to reduce stress. See where there is an imbalance, and even though it may take time and some readjustment, get yourself back on track. If you are working too hard, organize your time so that it includes rest and play. If your life is all play and rest, make sure you start getting intellectual and physical challenges in your life. If you aren't getting enough quiet time, set aside high-quality time for yourself. Creating a balance for yourself will diminish your stress considerably.

So, if you are about to pour yourself your fifth cup of coffee and it's only ten o'clock in the morning, or you find yourself twitching to go to the gym instead of accepting a lunch date, or you take on a work commitment that you know you haven't got time for, or you spend money you know you don't have or say something you will regret or do anything that starts to damage and interfere with your health, let the sixth principle of coffee wisdom be your caution: boiling causes bitterness. Don't overdo things. Balance and moderation in everything—yes, everything—is the key to a happy life. All pleasurable things must come to an end, even that cup of coffee.

:: Chill Out

If you are reading this book with a cup of coffee and your feet up, you are taking time to recharge your batteries and focus on what makes you feel good. But if you are reading this book and feel tense and anxious, the chances are you often neglect setting aside time and space for chilling out.

When you get stressed, the muscles in your body tense, and muscular tension creates unpleasant sensations such as headaches, tightness in the chest, difficulty breathing, churning in the stomach, difficulty swallowing. These sensations trigger more tension, and a vicious cycle is set up. It is important to learn how to relax in response to bodily tension. You may be able to do this by taking a coffee break, watching a movie, reading a book, listening to music, or playing an instrument. But if you can't relax, you need to learn how to take time out. One way to do this is to relax your whole body slowly, muscle by muscle. Start by dropping your shoulders, relaxing the muscles in your body and in your face—it's amazing how many of us frown without knowing it—breathing deeply, and gently relaxing. There are many tapes on the market that can help you through the process. You could also try counting to ten before you react, or repeat some positive affirmation to yourself, like "I am in control."

Techniques such as meditation and yoga can also have astonishing results if you are stressed and tense. Try this simple routine: choose a focus word or phrase—for example, "peace" or "happy." Sit quietly, and relax your body by tensing and then relaxing your muscles and breathing deeply. Say the focus word every time you exhale. If you lose concentration, simply return your thoughts to the word. Try this for just five minutes at first, and then gradually increase the amount of time. Do the routine at least once a day.

Don't expect relaxation to be easy. Relaxing for some of us is a skill that has to be practiced. You may feel peculiar or uncomfortable at first if you are used to tension. Don't worry about this;

just accept that it will take time before you feel comfortable. Make sure that you are breathing deeply and are not practicing when you are hungry, full, or overtired. Make your environment conducive to relaxation. If you get a cramp, ease the tension by rubbing the painful area gently. If you fall asleep easily, you might want to avoid lying down.

Expect your relaxation to be interrupted by stressed out thoughts. The best way to deal with them is not to dwell on them. Just accept that they will drift into your mind from time to time, and then refocus on your relaxation. If you don't feel the benefit right away, don't give up or try too hard. Just let the sensation of relaxation happen. Correct breathing will help.

Deep, slow breathing through your nose rather than your mouth, allowing your abdomen to move, can calm both body and mind and help you cope with stress. Simple yoga breathing exercises may also help—for example, try breathing in slowly through the nose while counting to five, holding your breath for a count of five, breathing out slowly through the nose for a count of five, waiting a count of five, and repeating as often as you like. Concentrating on breathing and counting can be wonderfully calming for your mind, while the regular breathing will calm your body.

When you are stressed, you may hyperventilate or breathe rapidly. This rapid breathing is a natural response to stress or exertion. It uses the upper part of the lungs and results in too much oxygen intake. Everyone hyperventilates when they are tense or are exercising. We breathe faster to give our muscles oxygen for increased activity to relieve the stress. Rapid breathing isn't a problem if it is short term, but it is if it becomes habitual. It results in too much oxygen being taking into the bloodstream, upsetting the oxygen-carbon dioxide balance and causing unpleasant physical symptoms like tingling hands or face, muscle cramps, dizziness, fatigue, and aches and pains.

These symptoms can be quite alarming, and they can trigger another cycle of stress. It is easy to learn how to breathe correctly when you are anxious. Avoid breathing from your upper chest, and avoid gulping or gasping. When you first try to breathe correctly you might want to lie down to feel the difference between deep breathing and shallow breathing.

First, exhale as much as you can. Then, inhale gently and evenly through your nose, filling your lungs completely so that your abdominal muscles move outward. Then, exhale slowly and fully. Repeat this, trying to get a rhythm going. You might want to aim to take ten breaths a minute. If you are not getting enough air, return to breathing that is normal for you. Then, try increasing the length of one breath, breathing out fully, then in fully, then out again. If that breath felt comfortable, try another one. To get a rhythm going, it's important not to try hard but to cooperate as easily as you can with your breathing muscles. If you practice correct breathing every time you feel worried or anxious, you will find that it gets easier and easier to breathe deeply instead of rapidly.

Relaxation techniques like those mentioned above give you the space and time to put things into perspective. They encourage you to find that essential balance in life between body, mind, heart, and soul.

:: Balancing Body, Mind, Heart, and Soul

Voltaire was said to have consumed fifty cups of coffee a day. Coffee may or may not have played a role in his creative output but, if the reports of his coffee addiction are true, he probably had digestive trouble, not to mention insomnia, nervousness, and, of course, chronic stress.

::COFFEE BOX:

Notorious Coffee Drinkers::

Celebrated coffee drinkers include Voltaire, Louis XIV of France, Napoleon, J. S. Bach, composer of the *Coffee Cantata*, and Beethoven. "At breakfast Beethoven drank coffee . . . . Coffee seems to have been the nourishment with which he could least dispense and in his procedure with regard to preparation he was (most) careful . . . . Sixty beans to a cup was the allotment and the beans were often counted out exactly, especially when guests were present." Anton Schindler

Gustavus III of Sweden was also an enthusiast. Observing the effects of tea and coffee drinking, respectively, on a pair of twins, he concluded that coffee was healthier because the tea twin died first, aged 83.

The greatest coffee drinker, though, has to be Honoré de Balzac. He was one of France's most prolific authors and achieved this feat by sleeping only two hours a night and drinking over sixty cups of coffee a day.

Coffee drinking can be an area of life where it is easy to get things out of proportion. It's not hard to see why. You enjoy coffee. It makes you feel good. So why not drink more and more of it? We all know those magical moments when only a cup of coffee will do, but too much coffee can make you feel jumpy by day and wakeful by night. To really enjoy your coffee, you need to know that it isn't going to harm your health. Coffee is a treat to be enjoyed once or twice a day. Drink any more than that, and it isn't a treat anymore.

Applying the sixth principle of coffee wisdom is all about being responsible and caring for your mind, body, heart, and soul. It is about getting the balance in your life right. A balanced approach to life, taking care to avoid extremes, is the key element of a happy life. Think of a coffee plant. It needs the warm tropical temperatures by day, but it also needs an altitude that makes the nights cool, slowing down the growth of the plants and allowing the coffee to develop its finest flavor. Too much sunlight or too much moisture isn't good. Too little will also destroy it. So, what you need is a balanced environment to ensure the plant's healthy growth. In much the same way in your life, too much or too little of any one thing can have destructive effects.

The ancient Greeks' famous saying, "nothing overmuch," reminds us of the importance of balance. To perform at your peak, you need to strive for balance in all areas of your life.

:: Simmer, Don't Boil

Balance is absolutely crucial if you want to deal more effectively with life. If you are not doing the best for yourself, it's like pouring boiling water on your coffee. It doesn't matter how special the coffee beans are, your drink will taste bitter. But if you get the water temperature right, it will taste perfect. The coffee wisdom feel-good tips that follow are all about regularly renewing and strengthening the four key areas in your life: body, mind, heart, and soul.

> **Body:** Decide to eat well. You don't have to cut out everything you enjoy as long as you remember the principle of balance. Try the 80–20 rule. Eat healthily 80 percent of the time, and you can have your cake and eat it and your coffee and drink it 20 percent of the time. Focus on including more healthy food in your diet (lots of vegetables, fruit, high-fiber carbohydrates, and an adequate amount of protein plus lots of water to clear out toxins).

> Get regular exercise. Keep your fitness goals realistic. If you haven't exercised for a while, try ten minutes three times a week and build up from there. Small achievements will develop your motivation to increase your exercise, and once you start to feel better and enjoy the benefits, there will be no stopping you.

Sleep well. You need to feel rested and refreshed to enjoy life. Make sure you get enough quality sleep—most of the time. It's best to avoid coffee, heavy meals, and exercise at least two hours before you go to bed unless, of course, you are cramming for an exam, have been invited to a New Year's Party, or are on a hot date!

Mind: Education doesn't stop when you leave school. Keep your mind active by learning and discovering all the time. The next time you have a coffee, write down all kinds of things you may be good at. You may have a talent for reading, writing, or speaking. You may have a gift for creativity or helping others, or you may have a good memory, or organizational, music, or leadership skills. It doesn't matter where your interests lie. When you do something you enjoy, it's fun, it sharpens your mind, and it makes you feel good about yourself.

Heart: Use your coffee break, or anytime when you get a moment to reflect and relax, to ask yourself, "What am I feeling?" "Why does this make me feel a certain way?" "Does this feel good?" "Does this feel bad?" This will help you become more aware of your feelings and help you recognize your needs.

And when everything seems to be going downhill, keep your heart healthy and strong by laughing. Sometimes life serves you a terrible cup of coffee, and there is nothing you can do about it, so you may as well laugh. Learn to laugh at yourself or grin and bear it when strange or stupid things happen to you, because they will.

Soul: To feed your soul you need to base your life on positive values. Honesty, respect, love, loyalty, and responsibility are values that nourish the soul and keep your life on track. There are many more positive values, and your heart will easily recognize them. To grasp why these values are important, imagine your life based on their opposites. It's impossible to make coffee taste good if the beans aren't top quality, and it's impossible to be happy through dishonesty, hate, or anger. Living in accord with your values will give you the inner strength and resolve you need to lead a balanced and happy life.

::COFFEE BOX: A Question of Taste::

Coffee experts explore the world of taste and use terms that are lost on the rest of us, but they really are quite easy to understand once you know the jargon:

Acidity: This means a pleasant sharpness on the tongue, rather like dry, white wine. It can be fruity as in Kenyan coffees or metallic as in Mexican ones.

Body: This means the imaginary sense of weight of a liquid on the tongue. A full-bodied coffee, such as Java, would feel heavier than a light-bodied one.

Earth: This is a rather unpleasant, musty taste.

Rioy: This means a hard, almost medicinal or iodine taste favored in the eastern Mediterranean.

Gamey: This is a pleasant curdled flavor similar to that of yogurt in relation to milk, sometimes found in Ethiopian or Arabian flavors.

Rubbery: The distinctive coarse flavor of Robusta coffees.

Green: The harsh grassy flavor in coffee that has not been fully roasted or that has been incorrectly processed.

Well-balanced: This is a state in which the qualities of body, acidity, and flavor are in harmony so that no one element predominates at the expense of another.

:: Get Time on Your Side

The ability to manage time is essential for a balanced life. If you lead a busy life and don't organize your time, then sooner or later your busyness will overwhelm you. You won't have any fun at all because you are worrying about what you "should" or "could" or "ought" to do. Happily, you can correct this imbalance with an easy solution—time management. You don't have to stop doing all the things you enjoy; you just need to make the best use of your time. If your time is valuable to you, then start to manage it and put a value on your time and effort. You will feel good about yourself, and others will treat you with more respect. Here are some time management tips:

Write things down. Write down a list of all the things that you think that you need to do. Use a notebook, diary, or bulletin board. Then don't file your to-do list away; make sure you look at it daily.

Prioritize. This is the important bit. Prioritize your list. Do you really need to do everything on your list? If not, delete those items. Can you delegate some of your tasks to other people?

Do the hard things first. Do the most difficult tasks first at the start of the day. Don't keep putting things off. Stop procrastinating.

Say no. If you don't want to or can't do something say no, and say it once. Don't spend time worrying about the excuses you feel you need to make for saying no. You don't need a reason.

Ensure that you schedule regular time out for yourself every day. Don't make your coffee break the last priority. You are entitled to it and should not take on more responsibilities to fill in the gaps. To be productive, you need sufficient personal time to reflect and relax. If you don't give yourself that time, you might start feeling out of control again. Research has even shown that regular down-time is essential for productivity. So you see, your coffee break isn't a luxury—it's a necessity. From now on when you feel tense, think coffee, dark hot liquid, steaming up to your nose. Close your eyes. Warm your hands around that coffee cup. Relax.

:: Don't Neglect Your Inner Being

Take a close look at all aspects of your life using this balanced and skillful approach. Whom do you spend your time with? Do you balance the company you keep? Do you spend enough time with your family, friends, your partner, or your children? Do you make an effort to meet new people?

Do you have enough time on your own? Don't neglect your inner being. Seek out experiences that reach and feed your soul. It can be walking by the sea, listening to great music, lighting candles, reading great books, enjoying a cup of coffee. In a sense, it doesn't really matter what you do as long as it gives you space to clear your mind and food to fuel that deep, most inaccessible place that is the essence of your being.

When we forget to pay attention to our spirits, we become nervous, stressed, and afraid. One of the most effective ways to calm your mind is to get in touch with nature. We are all creatures of the earth, and the world will offer us support and calm if we take the time to connect with it. Here are few tips:

Plan an escape. Plan to escape the town or city even if only for a few hours a week.

Take a country walk. If this isn't possible, take a walk in the park.

Enjoy nature. Take time to appreciate the wonders of nature, the color of the sky, the green of the grass, the song of the birds.

Slow down. Slow down for a while and enjoy the peace and quiet.

It is surprising how quickly you can restore yourself in these ways. Low self-esteem is often the result of trying too hard to keep up with the pressures of modern life and neglecting our souls. Take a nature break, enjoy the simple pleasures, and restore your self-esteem.

Another way to relax and feel calm is to physically ground yourself. Become aware of your breathing, and slow it down till you feel calmer. Close your eyes and breathe deeply, allowing your abdomen to relax and expand. When you are ready, open your eyes and bring yourself slowly back into the room.

To lead a balanced life with inner strength and self-esteem, sometimes we need to be able to stop doing and just be. Just being releases tensions and increases our self-awareness. Spend a few minutes each day in total silence. Turn off the TV or radio. Don't read a book or do anything. This will be difficult at first, so don't sit for too long. As you get used to it, you will be able to do it for longer and be able to balance your being with your doing.

When you spend this kind of spiritual time alone, you motivate yourself and you can see more clearly which direction you should follow. You also put yourself in touch with the people and the things that matter to you. You may feel close to someone you love who lives far away. Or you may feel gratitude for all that you have in life. You may also develop a sense of being at one with the rest of the world and its people, and through this feeling of oneness you may well come to assume more responsibility for others.

It's so easy in our world to say we can't help others, we haven't got the time or the money. We moan that we can't afford a new pair of curtains or that we don't have a big enough car. We are often so bound up in our own dramas that we forget how much we have to be happy about. Being aware of our good fortune changes our attitude from being largely self-serving to a feeling that is more real and responsible. And with these emotions, we discover a different kind of satisfaction, inner peace, and gratitude.

So, whether or not you consider yourself a spiritual person, every time you take time to enjoy your experience, a coffee break or a candle-lit bath, you are taking care of your soul. This is the real you, and serving it brings you inner peace.

Principle #7

Drink It While It's Hot

About Coffee:
Drink your coffee soon after it is made. Coffee can be kept warm for only about fifteen minutes over a burner before the flavor becomes unpleasant.

About Life:
Live in the present with an attitude of positive expectancy.

Believe in yourself, and spend time on what matters. Wake up every morning and smell the coffee. Live your life to the full, and savor every precious moment.

:: Believe in You

Coffee wisdom principle #7 urges you to live in the moment, but to do that successfully you have to believe in yourself. The quality that motivates and inspires all the other coffee wisdom principles is a strong belief in yourself and your abilities.

Every time you put your feet up and enjoy a coffee practice the feeling of being a winner. This winning feeling will overcome difficulties that otherwise might seem impossible. You've enjoyed the taste of success from time to time, even though they may have been small victories. Try to recall one of these and focus on it.

The incident isn't as important as the feeling of success and satisfaction coming from it. It doesn't have to be a major victory, like getting promoted or becoming a parent. Even a small one will do, like winning a game of darts, getting to grips with your new espresso machine or getting your Christmas shopping done on time. Try to recall a successful experience that happened to you. Fill your mental picture with all the details you can recall and relive the feelings. As you relive them, you will not only remember how you felt—you will actually experience feelings of confidence and success.

There is not one person reading this book who is living up to their full potential. People who study the brain believe that we use less than 1 percent of our potential. You have within you the ability to achieve far more than you realize. Rid yourself of the belief that you are born with or without something. Alter your self-limiting beliefs and improve your ability to excel.

Prior to 1954 everyone knew it was impossible to run a mile in less than four minutes. Then along came Roger Bannister, who didn't believe in barriers. He set a new world record. He broke through an attitude of self-limitation, and once he had smashed the world record, all over the world runners were recording 4-minute miles. Why did this happen? Because a long-held belief had been shattered. Of course, there are limits to how much we can achieve, but the reason we achieve peak performance is because we don't realize what our limits really are. Running the 4-minute mile is the same as achieving any other goal. It is our mental barriers that must be overcome first. If we strongly believe we can achieve something, we will.

The secret to health and happiness is to simply work at feeling good every single moment of your life. Feeling good comes from feeling confident about who you are and feeling that your life has a purpose. It is an inner conviction that you possess the answers you need for overcoming any challenges that come your way. Feel like a winner. Visualize with anticipation the way that you want to be, and your behavior will catch up with the mental picture that you have of yourself.

:: The Power of Thought

Coffee wisdom principle #7 reminds you that you have within you already a source of enormous power for change and creativity which you can tap into at any time and which you can use to address whatever it is that you are dealing with right now. To live fully and creatively in the present you need to discover the power of thought. Once you discover it you will never feel helpless again.

As we saw in principle #5, by improving your thoughts you can dramatically change your life for the better. Thoughts are like magnets pulling you towards what you picture in your mind. So it is important to control what you think. Choose your thoughts wisely. What you habitually visualize may very well become reality. There is only one person responsible for the way you think: you. You build your destiny thought by thought.

Your thoughts create the reality of your life. Your thoughts come first and then your life pulls you in the direction of them. If you don't believe that you deserve success and happiness and the good things in life then your thoughts will make sure you don't get them. Use your thoughts to change your beliefs. Start right now, this minute. Tell yourself you are good enough, clever enough, lovable enough. Play these thoughts over and over in your mind.

Send out good will to others. If you don't like certain people, try changing the way you think about them. Imagine them being your friends and helping you. It won't be long before you start to see results, as others respond to your positive, optimistic attitude and the things you want start to come to you.

Catch those negative thoughts before they have a chance to demotivate you. Have a good long think about how much you expect disappointment in your life. If the pattern has been embedded in you since childhood, you may need some hard work to turn it around. Like learning a new language or moving to a new area, it will take effort to get there but once you get the hang of it, you will be so glad you put in the time. You can get to work right now with a positive expectation that you can change your negative self-talk into positive self-talk.

Every time you tell yourself you are doing it all wrong, or always have bad luck, challenge it. Everything that happens to you, however disastrous, is a combination of experiences. Was everything about it bad? Was it all your fault? Could any good come out of it now or in the future? Am I being rational here? Does this really matter?

If you really feel pessimistic and think it is unrealistic to change your opinion try something like this: Instead of, "We will never be able to afford a house of our own," try "As far as I know there is no way we can afford to buy a house of our own—unless something unexpected happens." By adding the "as far as you know" prefix to your thoughts and ideas, you remind yourself to expand your mind to include that which you do not know. You also open yourself to the possibility that circumstances could change—which they often do.

If other people are shoving negative opinions down your throat, try the same thing. For example, if your mother tells you that you'll never do anything with your life, imagine her saying, "In my opinion you will never succeed." Then, you can remind yourself that her opinion is her point of view, and it's certainly not shared by everyone—least of all you. Things can always change for the better.

When a negative thought enters your mind, catch it before it takes over, like weeds in a garden. Visualize yourself pulling out a negative thought weed, and then picture your garden returning to its natural beauty.

One of the greatest sources of anxiety is our fear that we will never be able to do the things we want to do. Don't wait until the end of your life to figure out what you wish you had done. Don't let fear of death panic you. Let it motivate you to think about what you really want to do. Research on senior citizens has shown that those who are the most comfortable with their own mortality do not ignore it but prepare for it. Think of the things you want to do, don't let **what ifs** get in the way, and start making them happen right now. Remember, just as coffee only stays warm for a certain amount of time, your life on this earth is also precious. Seize the moment. Live in the now.

:: Live for Today

Principle #7 urges you to let the here and now, this moment in time, have your attention, your energy, and your commitment. If you can do this, you will truly be living life to the full.

Living for today requires you to trust that the past and the future will take care of themselves beautifully, without unnecessary attention from you. Understand that you have everything you need right here, right now today. People who are happy and successful believe with absolute certainty that they will have everything they need, even when life doesn't go according to plan. Bad luck is temporary, and things will turn out for the best. There will always be days when they doubt themselves but they will always return to the quiet, knowing that the world is a good place and their needs will be taken care of.

If you are experiencing difficulties, don't wait until things resolve themselves to find the positive. Find the silver lining now. Sometimes life offers unbearable heartbreak, such as the loss of a loved one, and it may take much time before we gain our balance. But when it comes to everyday difficulties, no matter how tough your day has been, you can always find something you are grateful for—your health, the love of your friends and family, healthy kids, good food and so on. The next time you feel sorry for yourself, are angry with someone, or are really depressed, try to focus on what you already have to help yourself shift into a more positive and grateful frame of mind.

Enjoy what you do every day. You do countless things in the day that you can think of as chores or that you can think of as enjoyable. Going to the supermarket is something that has to be done, yes, but while you shop you get some time away from work or home, some time to think, and a chance to make some healthy food choices. Enjoy the ordinary.

We know most days will be regular days. Our lives will have some highlight days that stay with us forever, such as family celebrations or personal triumphs, but most days are quiet and ordinary. Yet within these ordinary days there are many opportunities for enjoyment, many of which we don't even think about or appreciate. Don't waste any more of those opportunities and take time to think about the simple pleasures of your life. Take Martha, for example, who recently reached her 106th birthday. As she sat in her rocking chair, gently rocking with a twinkle in her eye as a journalist asked her how she felt on her 106th birthday, she said she felt great, because every day was special to her.

Enjoy life at whatever age you are. Age is simply unrelated to levels of personal happiness. Researchers conducted a long-term study interviewing subjects many times over thirty years. When asked when they had been the happiest in their lives each time eight out of ten replied, "Right now." You are never too young or too old to be happy—unless you think you are.

You have been given life, and with it you—and not someone else—has the opportunity to define it. You write your own life script. No matter what life throws at you, it is the way you respond that counts. You can merely hope for happiness, or you can create it right here, right now. You can live in the past or long for a better future, or you can seize the moment, enjoy and appreciate what you have, and live every day of your life to the full.

:: What Matters to You?

You've got a lot to do, and it's hard to find the time. Your work or responsibilities to your home and family take up the lion's share of your time. On top of that you've got friends to see, the dog needs a walk, the house needs cleaning, you need to exercise and so on and on and on.

Principle #7—live in the moment—can help. It's about living in the now with an attitude of positive expectancy but it is also spending more time on what matters the most to you. Principles 1–6 urged you to start working towards your goals and take appropriate action. Principle #7 is putting them first in your life.

Living in the present means spending the present moment on what really counts. It means being strong and sticking to what you believe is right. It means caring more about what you think of you than what other people think of you. It means saying yes to your goals and no to things that are going to distract you. It means putting first things first.

:: What Kind of Person Are You?

Are you a procrastinator? Do you put things off until they are urgent because you like the sense of crisis? Are you a pleaser? Do you try to please everyone? Are you afraid to say no because you don't want to offend? Are you a professional slacker? Do you hang out and relax all the time?

Or are you someone who puts first things first? You may not be perfect, but you take a look at everything you have to do and make sure that the most important things get done first. You plan ahead so you are usually on top of things. This doesn't mean you aren't living in the present moment. It means that you organize your time so that what matters most to you, such as your loved ones, comes first, and you always have enough time for that. You know how to say no with a smile. You take time to relax but know that too much relaxation can turn into a waste of time. Although it's a struggle, staying balanced is important to you.

It takes courage and guts to stay true to what matters the most to you. When the pressure is on, it's all too easy to say yes to familiar old patterns, even if they don't quite fit you anymore. Staying true to what matters to you means being willing to do new things, make new friends, and stick to what you believe in. It might mean doing something difficult in the present in order to reach a goal in the future. This isn't forgetting to live in the present, it's choosing what matters the most to you.

Putting first things first will take discipline. It's not easy to set priorities, overcome fear, and do things that are difficult because you are working toward a goal. It takes discipline to do something because you know it is for a greater purpose and because it will allow you to be the best that you can be.

So what's holding you back? Take the journey that you are meant to take! And remember to enjoy that journey. As principle #7 reminds us, the game of life is not about the final score but about the playing. It is about the present moment not the destination. The choice is yours. You can be a winner. And if you can live life fully in the present moment, if you can savor every moment, then you are already a winner.

:: Savor Every Moment

When you open this book, you have an opportunity to give yourself a wonderful gift. Let the here and now, this moment in time, have your attention, your energy and your commitment, and you will be living life to the full.

Check out what you are doing right now. Are you living in the past or wishing your life away? Today you need to deal with today. Don't let the present become a blur, a rush, or a muddle. Live in the present, don't just exist in it. Don't place your energy elsewhere. If you do, you won't live life fully. So, if you are busy living in the future or rushing to keep track of time, stop right now and say to yourself, "Remember, be here now." Instead of gulping down your coffee, really taste it.

Let today be everything, whether it is sad or happy, challenging or frustrating. Just feel today to the full. Breathe deeply and be present in the moment. Look at your life as it is today and enjoy what it is. Listen to the people in your life and see who they really are. Make this moment the best that you can make it. Enjoy yourself!

Let go of worrying thoughts, and appreciate and act in the now. The power is always in the moment. This is it. This is another precious moment in your life. Are you enjoying it?

::COFFEE BOX: Keeping Coffee Fresh::

The coffee bean itself can be kept in good condition for up to six weeks, as it is not ground until immediately before use. Rapid oxidation means that ground coffee has to be packed correctly in order to keep out as much harmful oxygen as possible. This can be achieved by vacuum packing it or using a valve, which allows out the carbon dioxide produced by the coffee but does not allow the oxygen in. Specialty shops resolve this problem by roasting coffee beans in the shops or nearby.

In the home, it is possible to slow down the oxidation process that makes coffee stale by putting the ground coffee or beans in an airtight container in the fridge or freezer. A cold temperature slows down the rate of oxidation, and an airtight container protects the coffee from picking up other aromas—something it is prone to do.

Never forget that coffee is a fresh product that will fade. Roasted beans will last in an airtight container for about a month. Ground coffee will be at its best in an airtight container for about two weeks, and in a vacuum pack it will last up to a year. And when your coffee has been heated and is ready to drink, you have about ten to twenty minutes to enjoy the pleasure, because much of its flavor will be lost if you reheat it.

Afterword

Now that you have read the seven principles of coffee wisdom, will you ever look at a cup of coffee in the same way again? I hope not.

William Blake, the English poet, saw the world in a grain of sand, so why not see it in a blade of grass, the branch of a tree, the warmth of a kiss, the joy of laughter, the magic of a perfect cup of coffee, or anything else that inspires and comforts you? Why not see the world as a place of magic, mystery, joy, and wonder?

:: The World of Coffee

"In a coffee house just now among the rabble I bluntly asked, which is the treason table."

—Christopher Marlowe, 1618

The coffee tree is a striking, resilient, and charming plant that stands out. Long skinny branches boast shiny green leaves, tiny jasmine-scented blossoms, and clusters of green and rosy ripe berries all at the same time. Inside each berry are two coffee beans tucked together with flat sides facing each other, protected from the pulp of the fruit by layers of parchment.

No one is really sure how it was discovered that berries could be processed into a drink, although legends abound.

One story is that an Ethiopian goatherd called Kaldi discovered the bean. Weary of searching for food, Kaldi's herd started to nibble the sweet red berries from strange bushes. Unusual behavior followed. The goats began to kick up their heels with an appealing exuberance. Witnessing this lively behavior, Kaldi decided to try the berries too and was soon singing and dancing. When he confided his discovery of the divine berries to a monk, the news was heralded at a nearby monastery. The local holy men welcomed the way the cherries kept them from falling asleep during prayers.

Another story says that a holy man Ali bin Omar al-Shadhili was banished to Yemen after falling in love with the king's daughter. In Yemen, he and his disciples ate the berries and cooked them and drank the liquid. They went on to cure the king's people of sickness by giving them coffee to drink. Al-Shadhili was pardoned and won an everlasting place in the history of coffee as patron saint of coffee growers and drinkers.

Whatever the truth, it is known that the best of the beans, Arabica, originates in the Red Sea area and that the beans may have been cultivated as far back as the sixth century. In the early days coffee was considered a food. The fruit was eaten whole, and it was not until the thirteenth century that coffee was roasted and became a little more like the drink we know today. Gradually, the rest of the world discovered the stimulating properties of coffee, and by the end of the nineteenth century, it had spread rapidly around the globe.

The first coffeehouse opened in Cairo in 1550. Coffee soon became a challenge to established religion, and coffeehouses rapidly became a place of subversion. A number of houses in the Middle East were attacked and closed. In 1637, the first European coffeehouse opened in England and within thirty years had replaced taverns as the island's social, commercial, and political melting pot. Known as "penny universities," they were places where any subject might be discussed for the price of a cup of coffee. A number of newspapers, banks, and insurance houses sprang to life around the crowded wooden tables and among the heady aromas of roasted beans.

Coffee's reputation as a mild stimulant has often attracted the attention of zealots. The sixteenth-century governor of Mecca, Kair Bey, banned the drinking of coffee and coffeehouses themselves, believing them to inspire irreverent activities such as singing and dancing. Unfortunately for him, he announced his ban to the sultan of Cairo, who adored coffee and rescinded the ban. Kair Bey lost his head shortly after.

The Turks also tried to prohibit coffee. First Suleyman the Magnificent and later Kuprili, Grand Vizier of Constantinople, banned its consumption. Suspecting coffeehouses to be hotbeds of sin, Kuprili ordered that everyone caught drinking coffee should be tied into a sack and thrown into the sea. Charles II of England shared this opinion and banned coffee for the stimulating intellectual conversations it led to.

Later, the storming of the Bastille, the first act of the French Revolution, was rumored to have started in a coffeehouse near the opera, and the Green Dragon Coffee House in Boston was a regular meeting place for the architects of the Revolutionary War. As the seventeenth-century haven for male networking, English coffeehouses excluded females. Women joined the government in their disapproval, and in 1674 a woman's petition against coffee denounced the brew because of the way it enticed men away from their homes. A year later, King Charles II tried to shut down the coffeehouses, but he was unsuccessful. It is also thought that the coffeehouses lay at the center of the Age of Reason, which ran from the English revolution of 1688 to the French Revolution in 1789—according to the Illy brothers in **The Book of Coffee.**

Coffeehouses declined in England but they continued to be popular gathering places in the rest of Europe. One favorite Parisian haunt was the Café Procope, which opened its doors as a coffeehouse in 1689 and over the years welcomed philosophers such as Rousseau and Voltaire. Tea was the favorite choice for most American colonists until Boston threw its great tea party.

The Dutch had introduced coffee in America in 1660 and served it in coffeehouses fashioned after the English model. These became rendezvous points for revolutionary activities against King George of England and his tea tax, where customers such as John Adams and Paul Revere brewed a potent cup of coffee and politics. The boycott of tea, the Boston Tea Party in 1773, and the fight for freedom established coffee as the traditional drink of Americans. Coffee gives the stimulus to clear thought and conversation, and it is no surprise that some well-known revolutions were fomented in coffeehouses. Never forget that as a coffee lover you belong to a grand tradition of free thinkers, revolutionaries, and independent-minded individuals.

Despite attempts to ban coffee, it survived and grew in popularity. But the next huge development did not occur until the invention of the espresso machine about sixty years ago. Unfortunately, few people knew how to service their machines properly, which is why coffee bars were quite drab places until the Americans and French burst on the scene. Prior to that coffee shops were featureless rooms in airports and stations when people were in transit. They served bland food and bland coffee. A warm welcome then to the American chains and French and Italian coffee bars who introduced espresso to the steam machine.

America is now the biggest consumer of coffee worldwide, and the espresso machine has restored coffee to its rightful place as an interesting, diverse beverage. Flavored coffees are also very popular, with varieties such as vanilla, raspberry, chocolate mint, amaretto, chocolate, and orange available. Iced coffees and frappaccinos and a wide selection of decaffeinated coffees complete the picture of America as one of the most exciting places for a coffee lover to visit.

Now there is no looking back. All over the world coffeehouses have become temples of pleasure for people to do what they have always done since coffee arrived on the scene: chill out, exchange views, and generate new ideas.

From its humble origins in Ethiopia, coffee has grown into a vast economic and cultural force. The coffee industry is one of the world's largest employers, with millions of people worldwide working in cultivation and production. After oil, it is the world's most traded commodity in terms of value, with over 70 million bags of coffee being bought each year, representing a vital source of income for many Third World countries.

Today, there is no escaping the fact that coffee is one of the world's favorite beverages, but as the seven principles of coffee wisdom show us, the art of making and drinking coffee is far more than a beverage, it is a way of life. Serenity. Tranquillity. Balance. Inspiration. It's all right there in your cup.

For decades people have known about the energizing effect of coffee, but today the habit of dealing with life's problems over a coffee even has scientific backing. Research has finally proved that a cup of coffee really is a good way to soothe away tension and boost your mood. But you knew that already, didn't you!

To Our Readers